Creating your own Web page

Michel Dreyfus

With additional material by
Rob Young

GW00703325

Prentice
Hall

An imprint of **Pearson Education**

PEARSON EDUCATION LIMITED

Head Office:
Edinburgh Gate
Harlow
Essex CM20 2JE
Tel: +44 (0)1279 623623
Fax: +44 (0)1279 431059

London Office:
128 Long Acre
London WC2E 9AN
Tel: +44 (0)20 7447 2000
Fax: +44 (0)20 7240 5771

First published in Great Britain 2000

© Pearson Education Limited 2000

First published in 1998 as
Se Former en 1 Jour: Créer votre page Web
by CampusPress France
19, rue Michel Le Comte
75003 Paris
France

Library of Congress Cataloging in Publication Data
Available from the publisher.

British Library Cataloguing in Publication Data
A CIP catalogue record for this book can be obtained from the British Library.

ISBN 0-13-021253-9

10   9   8   7   6   5   4   3

Translated and typeset by Berlitz, Hertfordshire.
Printed and bound in Great Britain by Redwood Books Ltd, Trowbridge.

The publishers' policy is to use paper manufactured from sustainable forests.

Table of Contents

Introduction

One of the major reasons for the increasing popularity of the Internet is, without doubt, the Web and the attraction and diversity of the sites which it offers. Once you have seen several dozen, you will most likely want to join in yourself and offer your own Web page. On a technical level, there are no great difficulties to be overcome. More often it is ideas, their expression and implementation, which will cause problems from the moment you actually want to attract visitors.

This book is designed to guide you through the setting up of personal Web pages. And we deliberately use the word "personal" to imply a number of factors not encountered in setting up Web pages in a professional context, whether in terms of hardware or design.

HTML

It is impossible to talk about Web pages without saying the magic letters "H-T-M-L", which stand for HyperText Markup Language. Although HTML is a descendant of SGML, the page description language reserved for a special order of followers of the UNIX sect, it is a debased child, which has gained in strength by renouncing the purity of its origins, as is usually the case with genetics.

In reality, it is more a type of style sheet similar to what we find in modern word processors such as Microsoft Word or WordPerfect, except that HTML deals more with the structure of the document and the rendering of different parts of a text (whether illustrated or not) than to its reproduction in a fashion as close as possible to that imagined by the author. For example, the *relative* importance of the titles and sub-titles of your pages will be respected, but it is the user who will decide the font in which these will be displayed. The way in which the entire page will appear to the user will differ according to the type of screen he is using (size, resolution, number of colours). In other words, you cannot hope for a faithful reproduction of what you as a Web author planned.

WHAT YOU HAVE AND WHAT YOU KNOW

You own a PC running Windows (3.x, 95, 98 or even NT) and you know how to use the essential commands. You already have a subscription with an access provider and some experience of the Internet. As for Internet software, you already have a browser, probably Netscape Navigator or Internet Explorer, which are the most widely used. You know how to transfer files by FTP and you have FTP client software such as WS_FTP or Cute FTP.

The term "browser" refers to software for navigating around the Web.

Your access provider allows you to store a Web site on its hard disk and allocates you sufficient space (1 Mb is the absolute minimum, 5 Mb will be more comfortable). If not, in Chapter 11 we will see that there are generous patrons who offer space on their servers.

And for those who swear by the Macintosh? When you view a Web page, its origins are forgotten and its structure is the same whatever machine was used to create it. The principles for writing a Web site remain the same, only the software is different.

You also know how to write solid text, and can construct sentences which have meaning and which can be understood unambiguously by those who read them. And you are capable of stringing together several paragraphs without spelling mistakes. Or else you have a word processor which uses an excellent spell checker.

What you don't have (but is not necessary)

You do not have a permanent Internet connection as do large firms or large teaching and research institutes. You must therefore have recourse to an external provider to *publish* your site.

You do not have exceptional artistic talent, and maybe you can't even draw. You are not a page layout specialist and you have never published anything, whether on the Web or in the world of paper publishing. If, however, you have some experience in any of these areas, it is no bad thing and can only be for the better. But it is not absolutely necessary.

You probably don't have specific HTML publishing software, or, if you have, you perhaps don't know how to use it. In Chapter 4, we will give a brief overview of some of the most recent software which can be an effective aid and significantly simplify the writing of Web pages. There is some excellent shareware and even some freeware. We recommend that you try several, then keep one and use it.

What you will find here

This book is not quite a course on HTML, but is more than a simple outline of the language. This is because, although we do not have the space to set out all the options for each HTML command, we wish to go further than HTML itself, showing you everything which relates to it: how to draw up a Web page, why to use one command rather than another, what to avoid, how to host and reference your page, etc.

To get you up and running, we have broken down our overview as follows:

- **Chapter 1**. Contents and container. Choice of subject. Who to write for? General principles for a Web site. Beware of copyright! Behaviour of browsers.

- **Chapter 2**. General organisation of a Web page. Principles of page layout and navigation.

- **Chapter 3**. HTML Basics. Page divisions. Paragraphs, character entities, etc.

- **Chapter 4**. Brief overview of some of the many HTML editors and checkers.

- **Chapter 5**. Lists, images, sounds, multimedia ... considered and appropriate use.

- **Chapter 6**. Everything that you ever wanted to know about links but were afraid to ask.

- **Chapter 7**. Tables and everything textual and graphical that they allow to be displayed.

- **Chapter 8**. How to soup up your site: image maps, counters, forms and frames.

- **Chapter 9**. General summary: example of a complete Web site.

- **Chapter 10**. Gadgets and innovations: Java, JavaScript, ActiveX, style sheets, Dynamic HTML.

- **Chapter 11**. And now that your work of art is complete, install it and make it known to the whole world.

- **Chapter 12**. To top it all off, a collection of great addresses, interesting texts, publications, software, pages of interest, etc.

A FEW WORDS BEFORE STARTING

It is not our intention to make you an HTML pro. Our aim is simply to get you up and running as fast as possible so that you can comfortably write a well-formed HTML page. This is why we have chosen HTML 3.2, which is currently recognised by all browser software, as the basis for this book and not the latest version 4.0. This includes around a hundred tags and you may be excused for finding it difficult to make the right choice. What is more, not all the new features included in it are correctly interpreted by Web software.

The screencaptures which illustrate this manual are 640 × 480 for technical reasons linked to the format of the book (if they had been larger, their contents would not have been readable). Different versions of the two most widely used browsers (Netscape Navigator and Microsoft's Internet Explorer) have been used for this purpose. The operating system used is Windows 95.

Web site addresses that are cited were correct at the end of the first six months of 1999, but things being what they are on the Web, it is not certain that some of them may have changed by the time you wish to use them.

In order to facilitate their use and not to bulk up the text, most URLs of resources cited are listed in Chapter 12 (Useful addresses).

A URL is the address of an Internet resource. You will learn more about this in Chapter 6.

TYPOGRAPHICAL CONVENTIONS

In order to make reading easier, we have adopted the following typographical conventions in this work:

Web page coding and, more generally, programming language elements appear in a `monospaced font`.

Internet addresses such as **http://www.pearsoned-ema.com** (the site for Pearson Education) are in bold.

Pictograms placed in the margin indicate notes providing supplementary information, explaining a new idea or presenting a term that is met for the first time. The pictogram used indicates the contents of the note.

 These notes provide additional information about the subject concerned.

 These notes indicate a variety of shortcuts: keyboard shortcuts, "wizard" options, techniques reserved for experts, etc.

These notes warn you of the risks associated with a particular action and, where necessary, show you how to avoid any pitfalls.

This pictogram indicates an explanation of a term met for the first time.

Chapter 1

The contents and the container

THE CONTENTS FOR THIS CHAPTER

- Choosing your subject matter

- Attracting the appropriate audience

- Structuring your page

- Staying within the law

- Configuring for particular browsers

It is (almost) as easy to create a Web page which is empty of meaning and offers nothing of interest as it is to deface a wall with a shapeless, ugly scrawl. In both cases it is the same thing: you have nothing to say, but to make up for a feeling of frustration you make yourself heard anyway. If you have some artistic talent, the emptiness of your thoughts may well be less obvious, but those who arrive at your page, through curiosity or by chance, will, most likely, not want to return and if you get any publicity, it will probably be negative.

A Web page is a lot like vanity publishing. When your manuscript has been rejected by all the book publishers, you will always be able to find one who will agree to publish it if you bear all the costs of publishing and if they can make a considerable profit. In this area, the advantage of the Web is that the cost is practically zero. This is why the hard disks of many access providers have been pointlessly filled up.

CHOOSING YOUR SUBJECT MATTER

As we mentioned in the introduction, your wish is to create a **personal** page. Therefore, we will avoid anything that may have a commercial aim. In any case, setting up a good business site to promote a company or its products/services is for marketing specialists and advertising agencies. It is not for the amateur.

Some ideas to help you in choosing

Here is a non-exhaustive list of the areas in which you could have something to say:

- **Your life**. Try to pick something that is out of the ordinary. Have you done something unusual? Were you in some kind of dramatic situation (taken as a hostage, for example)? Have you met a celebrity? Is your job unusual?

- **Your ideas**. You may have strong opinions on certain subjects which you wish to share with others. Or maybe you belong to a political party which has not yet availed itself of the Web in spreading its ideas and you yourself wish to take the initiative.

- **Your personal e-zine**. If you have an original point of view on current affairs subjects, if your critical mind knows how to present certain events in an unusual way, if your natural curiosity leads you to deal with subjects which do not interest the general public, you could be of great benefit to your peers. In addition to being able to write you should also know how to maintain your reader's interest. News is like supermarket products: the use-by date is quickly passed.

- **Your latest invention**. If you are a budding inventor who is having some trouble with communication, here is a means which is more efficient than an inventors' fair for attracting manufacturers who might want to market your invention.

- **Your hobby**. From angling to drinking expensive French wine via restoration of vintage motorcycles, the field is wide open. The written press already includes many periodicals in this area: why not take your chances on the Internet?

- **A club of which you are a member**. This is an extension of the previous subject. If you wish to broaden your audience, get known, recruit new members, present the club in its best light, publicise its activities, how often it meets, the membership fees, etc.

- **Fan clubs**. From the latest fashionable folk, rock, rap or pop group to so-called 'cult' TV series, there is no lack of choice. It is up to you to get together original and interesting documents so that those who share your passion can find original and little known information on your site on the subject about which you all enthuse.

- **The latest shareware program that you have created**. If you are a computer buff and write programs which you think might interest others, this is certainly the fastest and most efficient way to get them known. Offer a downloadable demo version on your page.

And what if none of this excites you? Then browse for just a short time on the Web and you will discover subjects about which you have never thought and which might suit you perfectly. If pushed, why not create a Web page on searching for subjects on the Web?

In all cases, there is a key principle to observe: unity of subject matter. Keep to a main theme. The more original your subject (without being too personal), the more it will be naturally lively and attractive and the more visitors you will have.

Attracting customers

A Web page is like a shop window: if it is not welcoming and if it does not catch the eye, there is very little chance that the occasional passer-by will go into the shop (stay to read the Web site). Without being overbearing, your home page must be able to attract the gaze. And the visitor should not have to search for the subject that you are dealing with. On the pretext of making it pleasing to the eye, do not make the mistake of so many (bad) television advertisements in which, after 15 seconds, you're still wondering what they're trying to sell.

Some institutional presentations think that they have to be austere and important (i.e. boring), while others try to look like Times Square with flashing lights everywhere. Figure 1.1, the RSPCA site, is an example of good presentation.

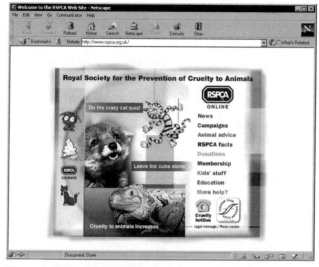

Figure 1.1: The RSPCA web site is attractive, but discreet

Some examples

Here is a list of some subjects already dealt with on the Web and showing a wide variety of themes and visual presentations. Most of these have been produced by amateurs. You will see that no subject is outside the scope of the Web.

- Everything about Sherlock Holmes:
  http://members.tripod.com/~msherman/holmes.html

- Alfred Hitchcock's "Psycho" dissected:
  http://www.geopages.com/Hollywood/1645

- New Era Motorcycle Club:
  http://www.neweramcc.freeserve.co.uk

- Centre for the Easily Amused:
  http://www.amused.com

- Chocolate Magazine:
  http://www.chocolate-magazine.co.uk

- The Ultimate Mr Bean Site:
  http://www.geocities.com/Hollywood/Studio/5866

- Philosophy at Large:
  http://www.liv.ac.uk/~srlclark/philos.html

- Thailand:
  http://www.escati.com/thailand_of_escati.htm

- Financial information and advice:
  http://www.moneymoneymoney.co.uk

- Thought of the Day:
  http://w3.one.net/~laura927/thought.html

- Cool Sites of the UK:
  http://www.stu.uea.ac.uk/outthere

- Steve's UK National Lottery Page:
  http://www.llednulb.demon.co.uk

- The RSPCA:
  http://www.rspca.org.uk

- 9D Web Graphics:
  http://members.aol.com/one9d

- The Complete 'Friends' Script index:
  http://www.geocities.com/TelevisionCity/Set/5799

- Computer hardware drivers:
  http://www.drivershq.com

- The UK Web Library:
  http://www.scit.wlv.ac.uk/wwlib/

- UK Airshow Review:
  http://www.uk-airshows.demon.co.uk

- The Oxford Street Live Cam:
  http://www.fujiint.co.uk/street

- Earth and Moon viewer:
  http://www.fourmilab.ch/earthview/vplanet.html

- The Prince of Wales:
  http://www.princeofwales.gov.uk

ATTRACTING THE APPROPRIATE AUDIENCE

If you publish, it is with the intention of being read. Which means that it is important to know your readers, who will not necessarily stumble on your site by chance. (See Chapter 11 on how to get yourself known.) You must therefore decide on the way in which you want to trawl: widely (targeting all Net surfers), or narrowly (targeting a well defined segment of Web users).

Which areas of interest?

You should adapt the way you express yourself depending on the targeted *readership*. You will not communicate with specialists and with an audience of "browsers" in the same way. If the subject of your Web page is the change in the use of the comma among the naturalist authors of the nineteenth century (and why not?), the tone of your expressions and the vocabulary you use will have to be refined. If you have chosen to target enthusiasts of fine pieces of engineering, avoid wording your page like this:

```
The company quickly decided on cubatures of
between 175 and 500 cm³. It kept faithful to
rim brakes and lubrication by simple loss,
but at the option of the purchaser offered a
model with a two-speed gear-box mounted in
the body of the Cardan shaft.
```

This was a vehicle with two wheels and a double spatial tube frame. The flat tank, fixed to one side of the frame, because of the mounting, always kept its angular shape. A simple tubular frame carried a suspension fork at the front with a rocker spring. It operated by a centrally rolled spring-loaded rocker arm. Aside from the motor controls the motorcycle was equipped with pedals. The rear mud-guard was also used as a heat dispenser.

Remember that one of the only things that people on the Web have in common is that they know how to use a browser and have some idea of the wealth that they can find on this medium. They are not all technicians!

STRUCTURING YOUR PAGE

A Web page is not a bar room chat. Your potential readers must have points of reference. With a printed journal, it is easy to spread several pages out in front of yourself. The Web restricts you to displaying only one page at a time, with the maximum size being the size of the screen. Of course, nothing stops a surfer from displaying several of your pages on his screen. However, since normal screens are often only large enough for a single page, displaying more than one is a tricky feat which well-informed amateurs will avoid. Hence the problem of *navigation* which we will deal with in Chapter 12.

This fragmentation imposes a certain discipline on the structure of a Web site. It is essential that your readers have reference points to find what interests them, to continue forwards or to go back. In addition to a certain discipline in breaking up your subject matter, we will see that this imposes certain constraints in the choice of layout. Although the idea of a page has nothing to do with what happens with a book or magazine we will see that there are basic similarities with the printed layout.

The title

We first deal with the title of your Web site (something catchy, if possible) which may include a brief summary of the subject that you will deal with. Remember that a surfer's exploration of a site will almost always start on the home page. It is up to you to give them the desire to continue their exploration. Look at the cover pages of magazines or the headlines in newspapers to get an idea of the means used to attract and then detain someone who is passing by. The title may be followed by a table of contents (or sub-titles) indicating the headings that you will deal with. The reader might not have any intention of reading them in the order that you have suggested, which is why you must create links so that by clicking on one of these sub-titles your reader immediately accesses the page where this theme is covered. (See Chapter 5 on the structure of these link menus.)

A link may be a word, a series of words or a picture on which a visitor clicks to display the corresponding page.

The main subject matter

The number and arrangement of the various sections which make up the main body of the Web page depend on the subject dealt with. Where possible, insert pictures, but make sure that they are relevant. Resist the temptation of putting in too many and remember that large pictures require more time to download which might be an annoyance to your visitor and cause them to look elsewhere.

The end of the site

How should you end a page? Not necessarily with a conclusion, for the simple reason that generally it is not required. Of course, if you tell an amazing and unbelievable story, it is here that we find out how it ends. If it is a club page you might be able to put a downloadable membership form here. But if it is a personal e-zine, it may well end abruptly, especially if its subject matter does not have links which are clearly established between one another.

Often, under a heading like "Other sites to look at", a list of other Web sites which relate to a similar subject is given. Etiquette demands that you ask the *webmaster* concerned for permission to include a reference to it. In reality, it is often a way of obtaining a link to your own site from the site you are referencing.

 A webmaster is the person who is responsible for editing or updating a Web site.

Signature

As in the written press, it is normal to sign your work. It is pointless putting your postal address but do not forget that you are on the Internet and that the Web is an interactive medium. For this reason, give your *e-mail* address which may encourage your readers to share their opinions with you. Avoid sending them a questionnaire. Primarily, because people do not like answering specific questions since they are asked to do so too often, but also because, on a technical level, this requires setting up forms and handling these is rarely accepted by service providers. (See Chapter 8 on forms.)

How up-to-date is the page

After a while, some information is no longer of interest. For example subjects such as weather forecasts or stock exchange rates are only interesting if you know on which day (and even at which time) they were published. The same is true of a page with the title "The latest IT news". As we will see, establishing a site is just the beginning. The site must be kept alive and new things added to it so that those who have discovered it return. In order to encourage them to go further than the home page, make a habit of clearly indicating when the site was last updated somewhere in the first screen. Figure 1.2 gives an example.

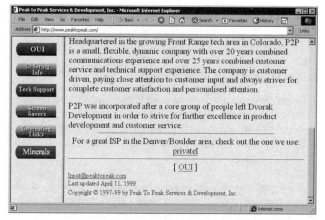

Figure 1.2: Note the indication of when the site was last updated

The counter

Very often, you will see a sentence like the following on the home page:

```
You are the 367th visitor
```

The visitor counter, when it is correctly set up, allows you to monitor the number of visitors to your site. However, be aware that if the counter is set up in the wrong place, the same visit may be counted several times. It is also possible to start the counter off at a value other than zero to give a false indication of popularity!

This counting system operates on the basis of a *script* on the server, but this is generally a standard script, access to which is offered by the majority of service providers. If yours is more strict in this regard, there are several public counters which you can easily access. We will return to this subject later.

A script is a short program which is located on the Web server and which carries out a particular function for a Web site.

Beware of copyright!

You can't put just anything on your Web page. As with anything that becomes public you are subject to the laws governing reproduction of intellectual creations such as: text, drawings, sculpture, photos, music, etc. Unless this work has already entered the public domain.

You are perfectly entitled to reproduce an entire poem by Keats, which became public domain long ago. The same goes for Beethoven. But if you want to post the first movement of the 14th Sonata (the famous *Clair de Lune*) on your page you have no right to borrow Daniel Barremboim's recording because performance rights are also protected. For safety's sake, it is better to record it yourself (if you are able do it, technically and, above all, artistically).

However, you have the right to quote, i.e. to borrow a short piece from an article or a work by a contemporary author. To know exactly where quoting ends and plagiarism starts, ask a lawyer. To reproduce an article or several paragraphs published in a newspaper, start by asking the permission of the author or the editor-in-chief of the newspaper, clearly explaining the use you wish to make of it. Often, and especially if your publication is on behalf of a non-profit association, you will obtain that permission, provided that you acknowledge your source.

You will find many sites which offer free images. The majority of these simply ask that you acknowledge them, which is not much to ask. Do not slavishly reproduce an image that you like from someone else's site, even if it is a personal home page, because the right to copy may not be passed on.

STAYING WITHIN THE LAW

A number of subjects may not be dealt with in public: racist propaganda, neo-Nazi theories, paedophilia and revisionism are among the things that you must avoid – and rightly so. Otherwise you will fall foul of the law and may be taken to court, as may your service provider. Most of these include a clause of this type in their conditions for hosting a web site.

CONFIGURING FOR PARTICULAR BROWSERS

Now let's move on to what your readers are going to see. Do not think for one moment that your site will look to them as you imagined it would. Depending on the browser they are using, the configuration options that they have chosen and the format of their screen, the results that they obtain may be very different from those that you hoped for.

The screen format

Figure 1.3 shows the home page of a site devoted to vintage motorcycles with a 640 × 480 screen displaying images. The main picture on the right is cut-off and you have to use the browser bars to see all of it.

Figure 1.3: A Web page displayed on a 640 × 480 screen looks squashed

The same image, displayed on a 800 × 600 screen (see Figure 1.4), shows every detail. This format is actually most often used and is probably the one which is most easy to view with high performance screens.

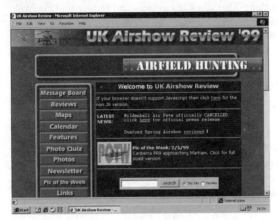

Figure 1.4: The same page displayed on a 800 × 600 screen appears complete

Displaying images

To save time, a Web surfer may decide not to display images, preferring to do without one of the main attractions of the Web. Figure 1.5 shows Microsoft's home page displayed normally on a 640 × 480 screen and Figure 1.6 shows the same with image download turned off. The difference in quality speaks for itself!

If the authors of this page had not used a device which allows an absent image to be replaced by a short text which gives a brief description, the navigation menus would have completely disappeared. Certain subjects, deprived of images, lose all interest. An extreme case is where the Web site is used to display a gallery of pictures or posters.

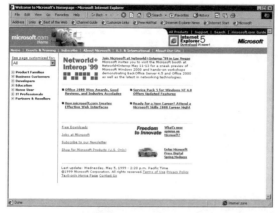

Figure 1.5: Microsoft's home page displayed normally

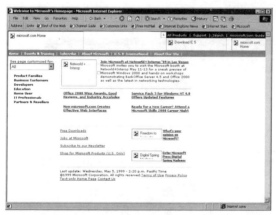

Figure 1.6: The same page without images

Choosing a Font

Finally, choosing a small font size (see Figure 1.7) or a very large font size (see Figure 1.8) will greatly affect the page layout and even navigation around a site.

Figure 1.7: A Web page displayed with a small font size

Figure 1.8: The same Web page displayed with a large font size

Using a browser which is too old

For these tests we have chosen modern browsers which recognise all the specifications of HTML 3.2. Why not HTML 4.0? For two reasons: firstly (as mentioned in the introduction) because the latest versions of the Netscape and Microsoft browsers are not able to support all innovations; and secondly because Web surfers, for the most part, remain faithful to a version that they know well and with which they are generally happy.

If your user has an "exotic" browser, whether because of using hardware which is not common, because of sticking with a browser discovered in 1995, or even because of not updating through laziness or ignorance, he or she runs the risk that a large portion of the page may not be displayed. Figure 1.9 shows a page viewed with Internet Explorer and Figure 1.10 the same page viewed with Mosaic, a browser developed by the American University of Illinois which was one of the first allowing exploration of the Web but which was quickly overtaken by more prestigious competitors such as Netscape or Microsoft. (In 1997 the university decided to stop developing the product, but to award licences to those who wished to do so).

Figure 1.9: A page viewed with Internet Explorer

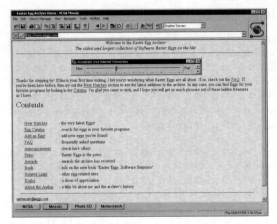

Figure 1.10: The same page (or rather what's left of it) viewed with Mosaic

The Web author's dilemma

All these things will probably lead you to ask: "For whom should I develop my Web site? For the majority or for those who are using the most recent browsers?" As is often the case, there is no easy answer. For our part, we think that it is reasonable to outline the average user: someone who owns hardware and software which is not too out-of-date (i.e. not more than two years) and who knows how to set it up without too much difficulty. This eliminates two extremes: those who still have 4800 bps modems and text-based navigators such as Lynx and those who have Internet Explorer 5+++ or Netscape Super Navigator 6*** with a direct 2 Mbps connection to the Internet.

Whatever the case, avoid putting a message in your home page like the one shown in Figure 1.11 showing that your page has been "optimised for" such and such a browser. This implies that you are incapable of setting up a Web site that everyone can view satisfactorily. Or worse still, that you have been paid by a software developer to promote its browser.

*Figure 1.11: Avoid this type of message on your home page;
generally it's an admission of powerlessness*

For the purpose of this book we therefore define the average user
as someone who uses Netscape Navigator or Internet Explorer
version 3 or more recent and is equipped with a 28,800 bps modem.
This configuration allows reasonably-sized images to be
downloaded in a reasonable time.

Chapter 2

Navigating around a Web page

THE CONTENTS FOR THIS CHAPTER

- Organising your page

- A practical approach to organisation

- Advice on page layout

The expression "Web page" is misleading because the idea of a page has little to do with a page of a newspaper or book. With these media, it is the format of the paper which determines what the page may contain and, whether you buy your newspaper in London or Birmingham, or whether you read it seated on a bench or on the Underground, the actual, physical page will always contain the same information.

> *A Web page is the part of a Web site which may be displayed on a screen.*
>
> *A Web site is a group of Web pages dealing with a particular subject.*

ORGANISING YOUR PAGE

We have shown in the previous chapter that things are quite different on the Web because of the wide range of hardware, systems and configuration options. One of the major drawbacks is the disappearance of conventional reference points: pagination, table of contents, index. And in the same way that you can read such and such a chapter of a book without necessarily following the natural order, with a Web site you must be able to get to the section which you are interested in without having to "flick through" everything that comes before it.

On the other hand, the linking of Web pages is not necessarily sequential as is the case for the pages of a book. If you assume that each section of the site is represented by a separate file, there are several means of organisation, which we will briefly consider.

Sequential organisation

This is shown in Figure 2.1. Aside from certain special cases, this way of organising the site, which copies the written form, should be avoided, because you can only access a particular section by moving through all those which precede it. It is very restrictive for the reader, who is confined to the route imposed by the author and cannot escape in a direction which is more suitable. Besides, there is no real need for this structure: a single page would be quite adequate.

The advantage of having several short pages as opposed to one long page is to be able to use the Next Page and Previous Page commands of the browser to go forwards and backwards in a site where there is no other way of navigating.

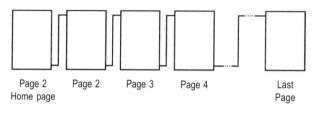

| Page 2 | Page 2 | Page 3 | Page 4 | Last |
| Home page | | | | Page |

Figure 2.1: Sequential organisation (like a book) of a Web site

Centralised organisation

This organisation, as shown in Figure 2.2, is typical for Web pages: in the home page, various pointers (called *links*: see Chapter 6) allow the visitor to go directly to a given section using a menu. The only problem is accessing this menu from a particular page. A system of *frames* (see Chapter 9) offers a neat solution to this problem, but this function is not always recognised correctly by all browsers.

This problem may be solved by using pointers situated at the end of each page which return a visitor to the home page where the menu is located. This gives the structure illustrated in Figure 2.3. If the page is long (more than two consecutive screens), a second pointer is often added making it possible, at the end of the page, to return to the start.

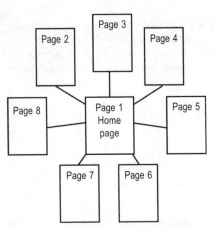

Figure 2.2: Centralised organisation of a Web site

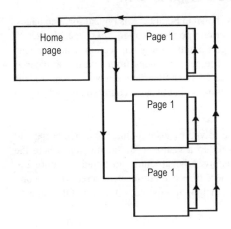

Figure 2.3: Centralised organisation with a return to the home page

▄▄▄▄ Hierarchical organisation

This is well suited to technical instructions or branch-type classifications such as those used in the natural sciences. But this type of organisation might also be found in catalogues: for example, a library organised by type of work, then by author and then by publisher, etc.; or a record library organised by century, musical form, composer, opus number, name of performer, etc.; or in gardening – vegetables, flowers, trees, seasons, months, types of cultivation, etc.

▄▄▄▄ Tentacle-type organisation

In a site which runs to many pages, if you're not careful you can end up with a structure, or rather a lack of structure, like the one shown in Figure 2.5. The author will have as much trouble making sense of it when updating as the visitor has when browsing.

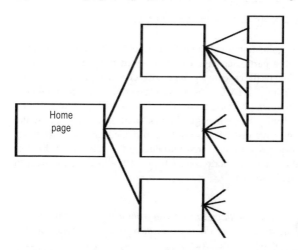

Figure 2.4: A hierarchical organisation

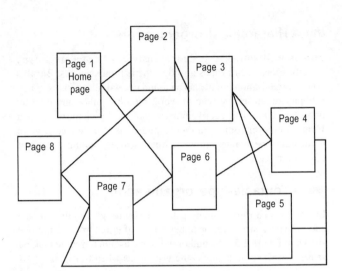

Figure 2.5: An uncommon branch-type organisation

Without going to this extreme, it is possible to have an organisation
in which a particular page can be reached from any other page.
This might be the case for a glossary of technical terms, for example.
Unfortunately, HTML does not at present allow an easy solution
to this problem, because there is no notion of sub-programs. To be
able to display a certain page and then go back automatically to the
page you have just left has not been provided for and no browser
developer has yet considered introducing this refinement. Frames
and, above all, JavaScript (see Chapter 10) allow this problem to
be partially solved.

*There is nothing to stop you from using a structure which
is a mixture of the ones we have seen. It is your site and
you are its architect.*

A PRACTICAL APPROACH TO ORGANISATION

Once you have chosen your subject according to the suggestions made in Chapter 1, it would be best if you did not throw yourself head first into the writing of your pages without first sketching out the way in which they will be organised. This is what the Americans call the *storyboard*, a term which is borrowed from the cinema. For this, paper and pencil are the ideal media. Followers of the shadock school of thinking (why do it simply when you can make it difficult?) might prefer drawing software for this, but it really isn't worth the bother.

This structure should clearly set out the sections to be dealt with on each page and, above all, the paths which allow passage from one to another. For a personal Web site, given the limited space available (in general around about 5 MB), it is not worth having a level of complexity which makes it necessary to set it out on a cork board with cardboard rectangles, colour threads and drawing pins which might be useful for some professional sites. Two approaches are possible here.

The constructionist approach

You have a perfectly organised brain and, like Beethoven who could "hear" his compositions despite being deaf, you are capable of seeing what your Web site will contain from A to Z in terms of how it is broken down. As a consequence, you have decided that you will not write a single line (or that you will not launch your HTML editor) until your plan is sketched out in every minute detail with all the links in one direction or another carefully set out, and every image and other multi-media file brought together.

Congratulations! you deserve an award. Then, once everything is finished and the last line written, you realise that the result does not match your expectations and the only thing for it is to start over again.

The experimental approach

This is the policy of small steps. You see more or less the whole organisation but, because you're clever, you prefer to start by planning one or two sections, writing or generating their HTML code and, without going any further, seeing with the help of a browser whether the result you have obtained matches up to your hopes. In general, this will not be the case and you will have to return again and again to the drawing board (in practice, five or six times). In this way you will be able to capture the tone and rhythm which you think are suitable for the subject matter you're handling. Once this is done, you can simply organise other sections based on this model.

This is the approach we prefer, by far. It seems to us to correspond better to the idea of a living thing that a Web site is, continually updating and starting over, than does the constructionist approach, which is too inflexible.

ADVICE ON PAGE LAYOUT

As we shall see, HTML allows a certain amount of choice in the font for text display. Novices who discover word processors hurry to use the largest number of fonts possible and so create ugly texts which are often difficult to read. What gives a tone to the contents is uniformity of presentation. Which is not to say that you should always use the traditional Times font. There are other fonts which may be well suited to personal pages.

Unfortunately, if your visitor uses a browser which does not recognise the HTML command for choosing a font or where the operating system does not have the specified font, he will see something completely different from what you, the author, anticipated. Therefore, in Windows, to minimise risks, choose from one of the standard fonts such as Times Roman, Arial, Courier or Line Printer. Whatever the case, don't use more than two fonts in your site, except in very special cases where you are looking for special effects. In which case, tell the visitor that to see your site under the best conditions he should install the fonts which you have listed. Then, if he is missing a few, he won't be too disappointed, and if the subject you are dealing with (and, above all, the way in which you are dealing with it) really does interest him, he will be able to get the fonts that he is missing and return to your page later.

Do not suggest that your visitor should download the necessary fonts unless you are sure that they are in the public domain, which is not always the case.

Chapter 3

HTML basics

THE CONTENTS FOR THIS CHAPTER

- Some HTML standards

- Starting to write your page

- Adding comments

- Commands relating to paragraphs

- Text formatting commands

- HTML and colours

HTML is the language of the Web. It is not a language in the sense of a programming language, but more like an idiom or even a dialect. As with any language, HTML has its own rules of syntax and spelling. We will not analyse these rules in full, but, after setting out some general principles, we will see how each of the most common HTML commands should be used.

HTML stands for HyperText Markup Language.

The most recent HTML editors boast that they make it possible to create sophisticated Web pages without knowing anything about the language. In some cases this may be true (allowing a certain exaggeration for advertising purposes), but we believe that it is useful to know the internal structure of the documents created, i.e. to learn some HTML commands. This is justified for several reasons:

- In some cases, you may wish to precisely adjust what the editor shows you and you don't understand the codes that it is generating (or it is not capable of doing what you would like). The only solution is to get your hands dirty.

- HTML is evolving faster than the editors. To use new HTML commands unknown to your favourite editor, the solution is to incorporate them directly into your pages using a basic text editor.

- Even the best HTML editors are not free of bugs. Fixing (badly) created HTML code is easy as long as you can recognise HTML commands.

SOME HTML STANDARDS

At its inception, HTML comprised few commands because it was designed mainly to handle text and to describe documents with a relatively simple structure. With the success of the Web, browser developers and, in particular, Netscape set about adding new commands to HTML to increase its flexibility and power. Under pressure from users and software developers, the official committee in charge of HTML standards, the W3C, finally recognised most of the new tags and this became version 2. However, Netscape continued to innovate and battled with Microsoft, which had just woken up and discovered the Internet and the Web, to offer the most varied commands.

These expansions were submitted to W3C, together with other suggestions for the creation of a version 3, but time passed and nothing was finalised, probably due to the scope of the proposed expansions, e.g. style sheets and handling of mathematical texts. In desperation, version 3.2 was announced in May 1996, dispensing with these two major considerations and confirming nearly all the changes suggested by Netscape and Microsoft. Style sheets are now included in the latest version of the language (4.0).

As well as several additional commands (dealing mainly with multimedia) and attributes, interest in which remains to be seen, Netscape Navigator and Internet Explorer (which comprise more than 90% of the browsers used across the world) recognise practically all the specifications of HTML 3.2. Not all the innovations included in HTML 4.0 have yet been implemented. When writing a Web page, you have to take into account this delay, the fact that not all users are going to rush out to purchase the latest browser on release and that you would like as many people as possible see it under the best possible conditions.

An attribute is an element placed in a tag or in a container tag to provide additional information to the HTML command in question.

STARTING TO WRITE YOUR PAGE

At the moment, you are invited to use the simple text editor NotePad which comes as standard with Windows. During the next chapter, we will study some of the many specialised editors which are available.

To demonstrate how to write a Web page, we will use a simple example which we have chosen. Figure 3.1 is a copy of the screen displayed by a browser to which the following file has been sent:

In this text, indentations and line spaces are used only to facilitate reading of the HTML document. They have no affect on what the browser displays, as will be explained later.

```
<HTML>

<HEAD>
 <TITLE>Your first HTML page</TITLE>
</HEAD>

<BODY>

<DIV ALIGN=CENTER>
<H1><IMG SRC="aladin.gif">
    My little e-zine
  <IMG SRC="aladin.gif">
</H1>
</DIV>
```

As you know, usually it is <I>on a flight of fancy</I> that I choose subjects that I wish to deal with in my pages. Therefore, do not expect logical links between the subjects I offer. Their only point in common may well be that they are well away from the current affairs with which the traditional media bludgeon you.

```
<BR>
<IMG SRC="cybds.gif">
<CENTER>
 <H4>Today I suggest the following subjects:
 </H4>
</CENTER>
<UL>
 <LI>Flowering of astilbes.
 <LI>Why <B>Hitchcock </B>never made a film
about
 <B>Sherlock Holmes</B>.
 <LI>The strange loves of the common
stickleback.
</UL>
<HR>
```

```
<ADDRESS>
 Your comments are welcome to
 <A HREF=mailto:jdupont@monmail.fr>
 jdupont@monmail.fr</A>.
 <P>
 This page was written on 19 May 1999.
 <HR>
</ADDRESS>
</BODY>
</HTML>
```

Figure 3.1: Your first Web page

To view a local HTML file in Netscape or Internet Explorer, enter <Ctrl>+<O>, then use the file selection box to select your file. Click OK to open it.

We will now dissect this short piece.

Tags

A tag is a series of upper or lower case characters, with no spaces, placed between < and >. Generally, as here, upper case is used.

HTML commands are represented by tags: <HTML>, <TITLE>, <BODY>, etc. Some of these tags are used singly, for example those that stop display on one line and have it continue on the next: <BR>. These are usually called *markup commands*. Most tags, however, are used in pairs. The end tag is identical to the start tag except for one difference: its name is preceded by a slash. These are called *container tags*. The command has an effect on the text placed between the start and end tags. Thus, the sentence

```
As evening fell, <B>the wicked man</B> arrived
```

will be displayed as follows:

```
As evening fell, the wicked man arrived
```

(The tag <B> indicates that the text should be displayed in bold).

Everything that is not a tag is ordinary text and will be displayed as such. Most of the time it is possible to embed container tags provided that the innermost container tag is entirely included in the adjacent one, and so on to the outermost tag. In the previous example, it would be possible to obtain a display in bold italic by writing:

```
As evening fell, <B><I>the wicked man</I></
B> arrived
```

or:

```
As evening fell, <I><B>the wicked man</B></I>
arrived
```

In the text, if you want to use certain characters which have a special meaning, it is necessary, as we have seen, to use entities so that they are not interpreted as tag indicators. For example to display the sentence

```
The <B> container tag indicates bold text.
```

you would need to write the HTML document as follows:

```
The &lt;B&gt; container tag indicates bold text.
```

Attributes

A tag may include attributes (some compulsory, others optional) which complete the meaning of the command. So, for the `<IMG>` command which allows insertion of an image, the `SRC=` attribute (which indicates the image file to be inserted) is compulsory. On the other hand, the `ALIGN=` attribute of this same command is entirely optional. Almost always, the text that follows the equals sign must be placed in inverted commas as in:

```
<IMG SRC="mypict.gif">
```

Separators

In addition to punctuation marks, which keep their usual meaning (with the exception of semi-colons terminating character units), the common separators – space, tab, and carriage return – are interpreted as a single space whether they are used once or more than once. Thus, the HTML text

```
As    far as is
possible
     you must
please

everyone.
```

will be displayed as

```
As far as is possible you must please everyone.
```

*The unit ** ** is called a non-breaking space. A series of several non-breaking spaces (, for example) is interpreted as an extended space (here three consecutive spaces).*

The two parts of an HTML file

All HTML files are located in their entirety in an <HTML> container tag comprising two parts: the head and the body.

The Head

The head is placed in a <HEAD> container tag which often has only one command – <TITLE> – specifying a general title for the site. It is this title which is displayed in the title bar of the browser. No other part of the head is displayed on the screen. In our example, we have:

```
<HEAD>
<TITLE>Your first HTML page</TITLE>
</HEAD>
```

You may also find a <META> command which is mainly used by search robots to automatically catalogue a site. We will return to this in Chapter 11.

The Body

The rest of the file is located in a <BODY> container tag. It is this part which will contain the various elements (text, images, etc.) which will be displayed. In our example, we have the following commands:

- <DIV> which indicates a sub-division of the body to which specific formatting is to be applied, i.e. alignment (here, centring).

- <H1> which indicates a top-level title (there are 6).

- <IMG> which indicates that an image is to be included.

-
 which is the equivalent of a carriage return (the display continues on the next line).

- <P> which is the same as <BR>, with the addition of a line space.

- `<UL>` and `<LI>` which are used to construct a bulleted list.

- `<ADDRESS>` which generally contains information about the identity of the text and the author.

- `<A>` which indicates a link (here for sending an electronic message to the author).

- `<HR>` which inserts a horizontal line (a *rule*) into the text.

These commands will be studied later, either in this chapter or in a later chapter.

The `<BODY>` ... `</BODY>` container tags themselves accept many attributes, three of which are particularly useful:

- `BACKGROUND=name of image file` which allows wallpaper to be displayed as a background. The background is defined by a small image reproduced as a mosaic across the whole screen. Figure 3.2 shows the result obtained with an image with a format of 160×100 pixels.

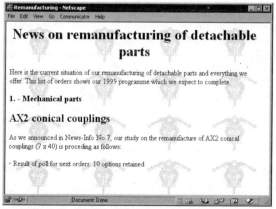

Figure 3.2: How to decorate the background with wallpaper

- `BGCOLOR=name of colour` which allows the background to be coloured with a single colour.

- `TEXT=name of colour` which defines the colour of the text for the entire document.

We will look at these more closely at the end of the chapter.

What happens to unknown commands

If you make a mistake when entering an HTML command (by writing `<BODI>` instead of `<BODY>`, for example), the browser will not run a diagnostic. It will simply ignore the command and try to move to the next command which it understands. This can sometimes cause surprises: strange interpretation of certain commands or disappearance of part of the text, for example. Hence the importance of HTML editors which automatically construct commands according to the layout information that you give them and thus avoid errors of this type.

Placing the commands

It is not necessary to place HTML commands (or at least the start tag of a container tag) at the start of a line, but it is recommended in order to improve the legibility of a file when you want to make alterations to it. The following text, taken from our example and arranged in single file, will produce exactly the same result:

```
<HTML><HEAD><TITLE>Your first HTML
page</TITLE></HEAD><BODY><DIV
ALIGN=CENTER><H1><IMG
SRC="aladin.gif">My little e-zine<IMG
SRC="aladin.gif"></H1></DIV> As you know,
usually it is on a
```

ADDING COMMENTS

HTML recognises the concept of notes, which allows a command to be ignored (while perfecting a site, for example). All you have to do is surround the lines involved with the start tag < ! -- and the end tag -->. Here is an example:

```
<!--<H2>This text will not be displayed!</H2>-->
```

Automatic generators of HTML code such as FrontPage (which we will discuss in Chapter 4) make extensive use of these notes in the HTML files which they generate.

COMMANDS RELATING TO PARAGRAPHS

In printed text, a paragraph is a series of sentences preceded and followed by a carriage return. Here, we have just seen that a carriage return is interpreted as a normal space. You therefore need to use a special markup command. However, some formatting commands automatically introduce a break in continuity of text, producing the same effect.

▰▰▰ The <BR> markup command

This is the exact equivalent of a real carriage return. It does not contain any attributes. You may place several of these markup commands one after another to increase spacing between two consecutive paragraphs:

```
First line
<BR>
Line 1
<BR><BR>
Line 2
<BR><BR><BR>
Line 3
<BR><BR><BR><BR>
Line 4
<BR><BR><BR><BR><BR>
End line
```

Figure 3.3 shows how Netscape Navigator displays this example.

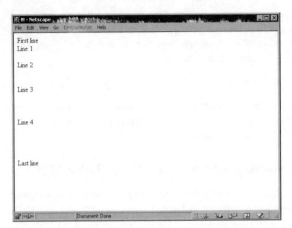

Figure 3.3: Producing line spacing of various sizes

▬▬ The *<P>* tag

The purpose of this tag has changed in the successive versions of HTML. Starting off as a container tag, it later appeared as an empty tag in HTML 2.0, then once again became a container tag in version 3.2 of HTML. For these reasons, browsers generally allow both types. It has the same effect as `<BR>`, but adds a line space as in the following example:

```
... this is the end of a paragraph
<P>
And this marks the beginning of the next one.
```

Figure 3.4 shows how these lines are displayed by Netscape Navigator.

Figure 3.4: The effect of the <P> tag

The <P> tag recognises the ALIGN= attribute with left (default), centre or right options, depending on whether you want the following paragraph to align to the left (normal), centrally, or to the right. Figure 3.5 shows the effect produced by the following text:

```
<P ALIGN=left>This paragraph is aligned to
the left
<P ALIGN=center>This paragraph is centred
<P ALIGN=right>This paragraph is aligned to
the right
```

Figure 3.5: Alignment of paragraphs with Netscape Navigator

The <DIV> container tag

This container tag is used to group various isolated elements (text, image, etc.) into a single unit which you wish to submit to the same processing (generally, alignment). It recognises the ALIGN= attribute with the same values as <P> (left alignment, centred and right alignment) and you can see the effect in the example reproduced above in Figure 3.1.

The *<HR>* tag

This separates two consecutive paragraphs with a centred horizontal line (*rule*), generally with a shadow. It recognises several attributes:

- WIDTH= followed by a number indicates the length of the line expressed in pixels. If this number is followed by the % character, it is a percentage of the width of the window.

- SIZE= followed by a number indicates the width of the line.

- NOSHADE (by itself) suppresses shadowing.

Interpretation of these attributes varies slightly depending on the browser used. Figure 3.6 shows the result obtained with the following text displayed by Netscape Navigator.

```
<HTML>
<HEAD>
<TITLE>The &lt;HR&gt; markup command</TITLE>
</HEAD>
<BODY>
... this is the end of a paragraph
<HR>
This is another paragraph..
<HR WIDTH=25%>
This is another paragraph..
<HR SIZE=10>
This is another paragraph..
<HR NOSHADE>
This is another paragraph..
</BODY>
</HTML>
```

Figure 3.6: Different forms of rule

Titles and sub-titles

We saw above that there is a `<TITLE>` command which is used to display the general title of the site in the title bar of the browser window. In the body of the page, there is a command allowing the display of six different levels of title, numbered from 1 to 6 in decreasing order of importance. For this, the container tag `<Hn>` is used, where n represents a number between 1 and 6. A title is automatically preceded and followed by a line feed. Figure 3.7 illustrates the relationship between these headings.

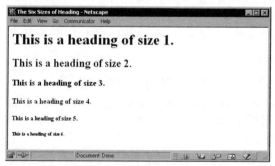

Figure 3.7: The effect obtained with the <Hn>container tag

In practice, levels 5 and 6 are not normally used.

Text formatting commands

Initially, the designers of HTML provided numerous ways of formatting text, but a great many of these have fallen out of use either because browsers have proved incapable of rendering their subtleties or because their use was not justified. The current tendency for these page layout facilities is to make use of style sheets, of which more in Chapter 10. In this section, we will only look at a few of the most common formatting features.

Logical styles and physical styles

This concerns one of the subtleties of the first version of HTML which has lost much of its importance. *Logical styles* describe the intentions of the Web author whereas *physical styles* have more to do with the specific way of changing the appearance of the text. In the two following sections, we will first give you the relevant logical style and then its physical equivalent.

Bold, italic and underlining

This type of formatting may apply to text of whatever length, from a single letter to one or more paragraphs. All you have to do is place the text to be affected in the appropriate container tag which is:

- `<STRONG>` ... `</STRONG>` or `<B>` ... `</B>` for bold.
- `<EM>` ... `</EM>` or `<I>` ... `</I>` for italic.
- `<U>`... `</U>` for underlining (no logical style).

Here is a simple example of the use of these text attributes the result of which is reproduced in Figure 3.8.

```
<HTML>
<HEAD>
<TITLE>Bold, italic and underlining</TITLE>
</HEAD>
<BODY>
```

```
<H2>Examples of common text attributes</H2>
Gracious king, you should climb <B>into the
branches of the tree</B>. Carry your bow and
<U>your arrows</U> up there: they may well be
of use. And stay silent: you will not have to
wait long
<P ALIGN=RIGHT><I>The Romance of Tristan and
Isolda</I>.
<HR>
</BODY>
</HTML>
```

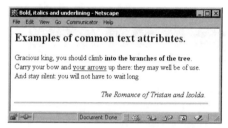

Figure 3.8: Bold, italic and underlining

Preformatted text

There is a way to give back to common separators (space, tab and
carriage return) their usual functions. This is to place the text which
contains them in the <PRE> container tags. Here, the navigator
will use a monospaced font of the Courier type. This is what is
called *preformatted text*. This was the method used to display tables
before the arrival of <TABLE> container tags (which we will study
in Chapter 7). Here is an example, illustrated in Figure 3.9:

```
<HTML>
<HEAD>
<TITLE>Preformatted text </TITLE>
</HEAD>
<BODY>
```

```
<H2>The Moon during the months of June, July
and August</H2>
<PRE>
 Month  | New    | First   | Full  | Final   |
        | Moon   | quarter | Moon  | Quarter |
 -------|--------|---------|-------|---------|
 June   |   5    |   13    |  20   |   27    |
 July   |   4    |   12    |  20   |   26    |
 August |   3    |   11    |  18   |   25    |
</PRE>
<HR>
</BODY>
</HTML>
```

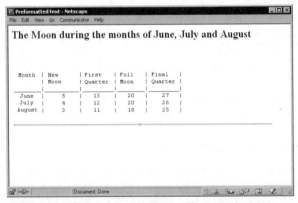

Figure 3.9: An example of preformatted text used for constructing a table

There are three container tags which allow their contents to be displayed with a monospaced font:

- With logical style : <CODE> ... </CODE>, <KBD> ... </KBD> and <SAMP> ... </SAMP>.

- With physical style: <TT> ... </TT>.

Figure 3.10 shows how they affect the following text:

```
<HTML>
<HEAD>
<TITLE>Monospaced fonts</TITLE>
</HEAD>
<BODY>
<H3>The container tags &lt;CODE&gt;,
&lt;KBD&gt;, &lt;SAMP&gt; and
&lt;TT&gt;</H3>
HTML has three container tags belonging to
the <SAMP>logical style</SAMP> to display text
with <KBD>a monospaced font </KBD> of the
<CODE>Courier</CODE> type. With the
<TT>physical style</TT>, there is also the
&lt;
TT&gt; container tag.
</BODY>
</HTML>
```

Figure 3.10: Several ways of displaying text with a Courier type font

Changes in size of the display font

There are two ways of changing the size of the displayed text. As a matter of interest, note the container tags <BIG> ... </BIG> and <SMALL> ... </SMALL> which allow the font size to be increased or decreased by one point.

More practically, the <FONT> ... </FONT> container tag accepts the SIZE=n attribute, where n represents either an absolute value (between 1 and 7) or a relative value (between -2 and +4) in relation to the normal size (3 by default). It also accepts the COLOR= attribute followed by a name or number for the colour. Figure 3.11 illustrates the results obtained with the exception of display in red (since this text is printed in black and white).

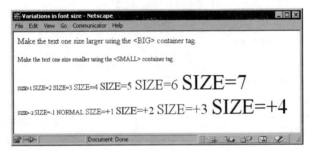

Figure 3.11: Various ways of changing the size of the displayed font

HTML AND COLOURS

HTML has two ways of referring to colours:

- **By their names**. For this, there is a list of 216 colours recognised by Netscape Navigator and Internet Explorer, taking into account the colours reserved by Windows. Some of them have poetic names such as *MistyRose*, *PaleGoldenrod*, *LightSeaGreen* and *PeachPuff*.

- **By a three number RGB code**. Every colour can be broken down into the three primary colours (red, green, and blue) at varying intensities. This brightness is expressed by a hexadecimal number between 0x00 and 0xff (0 and 255 in decimal).

If you would like the background of the screen to be *BlanchedAlmond* (pale yellow) and the text to be *RosyBrown* (faded pink, tinged brown), you could write:

```
<BODY BGCOLOR="BlanchedAlmond" TEXT="RosyBrown">
```

or:

```
<BODY BGCOLOR="0xFFEBCD" TEXT="#bc8f8f">
```

or a mixture of the two types of entry. Here, for the text colour, bc represents the intensity of the red component(188), and 8f (143), the intensity of the green and blue components.

All systems do not come up with exactly the same colour. From PC to Mac, from Netscape Navigator to Internet Explorer or from one video card to another you will sometimes see large differences. Hence the importance of testing your Web site on as many different systems as possible before offering it to the public.

Chapter 4

A few HTML editors and checkers

THE CONTENTS FOR THIS CHAPTER

- Choosing an HTML editor
- Checking your Web documents

It is possible to write an HTML document with a basic text editor, for example Windows' NotePad, but inserting the various tags quickly becomes tedious and remembering the exact syntax can turn into a nightmare. It is better to use specialised editors. Tucows, the well-known provider of shareware, has around 40, not including commercial products which are not offered on trial with the corresponding editor. We will review a few, in alphabetical order.

CHOOSING AN HTML EDITOR

HTML editors can be classified into three groups:

- Those which work on HTML text displayed in the working window. One or more toolbars and dialog boxes allow you to insert the appropriate tags.

- WYSIWYG editors which hide the formation of HTML, allowing you to work directly on the page layout of your document.

- Converters which use text created with a word processor, as far as possible converting the formatting into HTML commands.

We consider the automatic transformation of accented characters into character entities as an essential function of an HTML editor. We will therefore attach particular importance to this feature in the short analyses that you are about to read.

Finally, a fourth category has started to appear: converters using DTP files as a basis, translating as well as possible into HTML commands, for example NetObjects Fusion, available on the site of its developer (www.netobjects.com).

AOLpress

This is a basic WYSIWYG editor which has the not inconsiderable advantage of being free. Initially written by the American access provider AOL for its members, it has been made available to the HTML community. It allows you to compose a Web page while being completely unaware of all HTML tags. All you have to do is click in a toolbar or choose an option in the menus. Version 2.0 benefited from numerous improvements which have turned it into a powerful editor. It is used in a very similar way to a traditional word processor. Figure 4.1 shows how a page being edited is displayed.

Figure 4.1: Using AOLpress, writing a Web page is done without seeing the tags

An option (Tools/Show HTML) allows the HTML to be seen and, if desired, edited. The code is presented very clearly and its indentations favour manual amendments. One plus point is that character entities are generated automatically (see Figure 4.2).

AOLpress allows easy creation of tables and frames with the aid of dialog boxes and several neat features facilitate editing, such as that shown in Figure 4.3. You select an object (here an image, but it might be a list or a table) and leave the mouse stationary for a second. The corresponding HTML code is displayed in a window which disappears as soon as you move the mouse. Another clever feature is that you can change the size of an image with the mouse using the handles which appear when you select the image.

Figure 4.2: The HTML code created for our test

Figure 4.3: A practical way of checking coding: you can view the HTML code created for an object

An editor which is free and offers so many functions as well as being easy to use is very appealing.

Arachnophilia

Arachnophilia is not a commercial product, nor is it shareware or
freeware. Its author, an American by the name of Paul Lutus, calls
it *careware,* an idea which he defines as follows: the *customer*
obtains something of value in exchange for something the *seller*
wants. And what the seller wants here is: "anything except money".
Given the seeming generosity of this idea, you might imagine that
the product can't be that good. However, this is not a badly-written
bit of software, but rather a good quality product. Paul Lupus
explains his ideas in detail at the URL: **http://www.arachnoid.com/
lutusp/careware.htm**.

With this software we are working at the level of HTML commands.
When you click on File/New/HTML file, the editor creates an
outline page (see Figure 4.4) on which you can also view a menu
of the most frequent commands by right-clicking anywhere in the
page. You may personalise this if you wish.

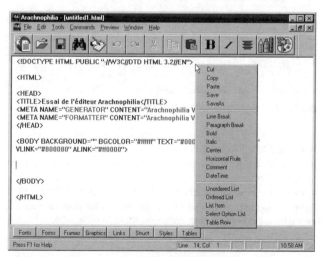

Figure 4.4: Arachnophilia offers an outline HTML document

Figure 4.5 shows the configuration options offered by the Tools/
Options menu. The buttons at the bottom of the page all allow
button bars for each of the HTML objects offered to be displayed.
To view the result, you can call on one of the four browsers that
you have previously defined, but you must change window
manually (Alt +TAB).

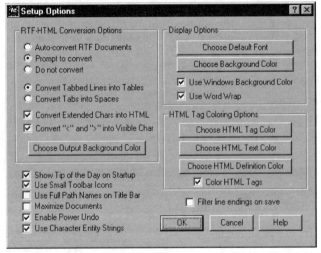

Figure 4.5: Arachnophilia's general configuration options

An integrated FTP server allows transfer of files to your host site
without quitting Arachnophilia (see Figure 4.6). You can also send
an e-mail using the e-mail program that you have previously
selected. There are means of including JavaScript scripts and Java
applets. Accented characters are not converted when they are input,
but you can click on Tools/Convert Extended Characters to convert
any which are contained in the page, should you need to.

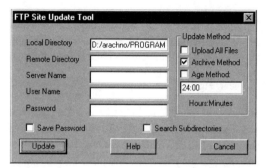

Figure 4.6: Arachnophilia has an integrated FTP server

On the downside, table generation is basic and is limited to creating an outline designed for two rows and two columns which is then difficult to customise. Frames must be created in the same way knowing exactly what you need to write and where you need to put it.

Finally, we must lament a certain simplicity in a product which is offered with such noble feelings. This editor should be placed just above basic text editors.

FrontPage

FrontPage is one of the real heavyweights. Microsoft has already scored a blow and the result is a software product which is very ambitious and fully featured. It is to the HTML field what Word for Windows is to word processing. It would take around 500 pages to give a complete overview, so numerous are its features. In addition, it is delivered with personal server software and a very powerful graphical editor.

This is an editor which is almost entirely WYSIWYG, but which still allows you to easily access the coding and change it if you wish. However, it is more than a simple HTML editor: it is a complete program for the creation of a Web site from the writing of each page up to installing it on the server, including automatic management of updates. It is, in fact, made up of two modules: FrontPage Explorer, which deals with the structure of the site; and FrontPage Editor, which allows the creation and/or modification of any page. You can switch from one to the other very easily by clicking in the toolbar. Figure 4.7 shows you how Explorer's screen is displayed.

> *When we say that FrontPage is "almost entirely WYSIWYG", it is because some options (the positioning of an image, for example) must be carried out with the aid of dialog boxes.*

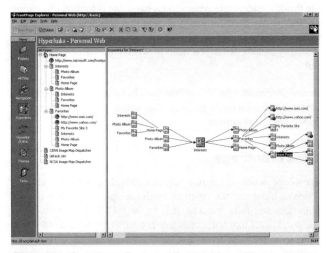

Figure 4.7: FrontPage Explorer displays the entire structure of a Web site

To create or change a page, you open FrontPage Explorer, which is the actual HTML editor. Figure 4.8 shows how a page looks without a single HTML tag in sight.

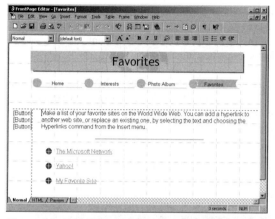

Figure 4.8: FrontPage Explorer is a WYSIWYG editor

You are able to view the structure of the HTML document created (Figure 4.9). The only drawback is that extended characters are not converted into entities.

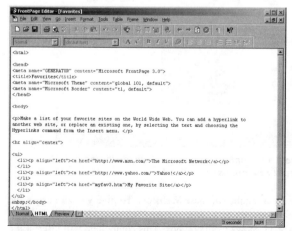

Figure 4.9: The HTML code created for the previous test

Many assistants come to your aid in the creation of pages. It is even possible to create some yourself. Generally, right-clicking on an object in the page displays a contextual menu allowing access to the object's properties (Figure 4.10).

The truly original feature of FrontPage is both its strength and weakness. This is the use of *WebBots*. To explain what this term means we can do no better than quote the definition given by Microsoft in its on-line help:

A dynamic object in a Web page read and executed when the author saves the page, or, sometimes, when a visitor accesses a page. Most WebBot components create HTML code.

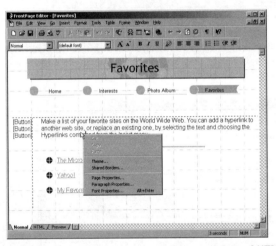

Figure 4.10: Contextual menus allow attributes of HTML objects to be precisely defined

There are a number of these WebBots. To give you an idea of the power of these objects, let's take the "Scheduled Include" WebBot. Figure 4.11 shows its dialog box. This component will insert a file in the site between two defined dates. In this way you can avoid continuing to announce a demonstration or a conference which has already taken place.

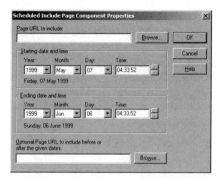

Figure 4.11: The "Scheduled Include" WebBot allows the insertion of an HTML file into a page for a time period set in advance

As practical as this innovation is, it requires that the host server contains *Microsoft FrontPage Extensions*. There are several versions, not only those for Windows NT servers, but also for most versions of UNIX. But, for reasons of security, many service administrators view this intrusion onto their servers suspiciously (at the very least) and will refuse point blank to have any foreign items on their machines.

That's where we stop our overview of FrontPage. What little we've seen is probably enough to convince you that it is directed more at the professional rather than the part-time Web author. However, considering its power it is not overly expensive. It is a particularly suitable product, for example, for managing an Intranet where installation of FrontPage Extensions will not create a problem and where its powerful site management features will work wonders. However, if you wish to look into FrontPage in greater depth, why not try *A Simple Guide to FrontPage 4.5* from the same publisher?

Internet Assistant

This is a set of macros written by Microsoft (and available for free, on its site, under the name WORDIA.EXE). These add HTML editing functions to the normal functions of the Word for Windows word processor and go as far as modifying and adding to the menus of this program.

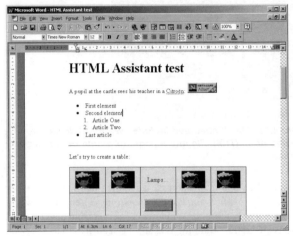

Figure 4.12: Editing an HTML document with Internet Assistant for Word

The choice between normal mode and HTML mode is made when you create a file by choosing the HTML.DOT template for an HTML file or when you start editing, depending on the extension of the file you wish to open.

Internet Assistant claims to be WYSIWYG and the result obtained is acceptable, as long as you are not too fussy about the layout. Figure 4.13 was taken from Internet Explorer with the HTML document generated. There is a preview button to automatically open a browser, but each time that you click on it a new copy of the browser is loaded which seriously clogs up the memory.

Figure 4.13: Internet Explorer display of a document generated by Internet Assistant

Internet Assistant allows you to import documents formatted by Word (or in RTF format), either by insertion of a file, or by copying and pasting. The conversion of the formatting into HTML tags is more or less successful.

Tables are generated by partially using the old Table menu entries, to which a few new commands have been added. You can access alignment parameters by right-clicking in the relevant cell and then, normally, on the Align command, which displays the dialog box shown in Figure 4.14. As for frames, we could find no menu command or button which allows them to be created.

In our opinion, the main advantages of Internet Assistant are that it is free and that it converts already formatted documents into HTML. On the whole, we prefer it to more simple tools such as AOLpress that we looked at previously. You must not believe that being used to Word will make it easy to use, because you will still have to familiarise yourself with the changes made in the menus and be able to identify the buttons and new toolbars.

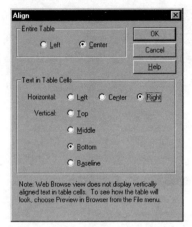

Figure 4.14: Alignment dialog box for the table cells

CHECKING YOUR WEB DOCUMENTS

Once you have finished writing an HTML document, it is only sensible to check it. The more sophisticated the tool used to create it, the lower the risk of finding errors.

Looking for errors

In the same way that after having written an ordinary document with a word processor, you spell-check it, it is good to check that there is no syntax error in a Web page. Of course, browsers are kind, and when they don't understand something that you have written, they always try to do something. But it will often not be what you expect.

Once you are sure that the syntax is correct, you then need to check that the links are sound. For internal links it is not necessary to connect to your access provider, because you can do the test locally. For others, it is necessary to carry out a 'live' test.

You must therefore carry out two levels of checking if you want to be reasonably sure of not publishing a site which is flawed.

Syntax errors

HTML is not as strict as the C programming language for which you know exactly what is and isn't allowed. There are many grey areas and the proliferation of extensions offered by editors does not help to clarify the situation. For each version there is an official document called a DTD (Document Type Definition) which is written in SGML, the ancestor of HTML. However, as you don't need to write your own DTD to use HTML we won't be referring to it.

The most common error is probably forgetting to close a tag. If the end tag is to be put at the end of the document, there is little chance of any harmful consequences. What use, for example is </HTML> if there is nothing else after it?

Another common error is forgetting the quotation marks. Generally, when you give a value to an attribute (SRC=, for example, for the <IMG> markup command), we have already seen that you have to put the series of characters which follows the equals sign between inverted commas. Most browsers are able to cope with their absence. However, if you put them in, you must use them in pairs. Forgetting to close inverted commas will probably cause some serious problems.

It is possible that you might invent an attribute which doesn't exist or that you misspell its name: VALIGN= in the <IMG> markup command, for example. Practically speaking, this will have few consequences because everything a browser does not recognise will be ignored. But you might be surprised that you don't see the page layout that you were expecting.

Most checking tools allow the possibility of defining the HTML syntax level that should be adhered to. The latest standard is numbered 4.0 and all the extensions added by Netscape and Microsoft are obviously not included in this.

Checking links

Here, the danger is that you may have misspelled a reference or a URL for images and pages. Some of these may be checked locally, but in a page of the type "My favourite sites" (where there may be around a dozen sites that you think worthy of recognition), it is good practice to make sure that the URLs have been spelled correctly and that these pages are still in existence. Anyone who has surfed the Web knows that an address is rarely permanent.

Testing the site 'live'

Even if all the previous tests have proved successful, you have still not finished. In the same way as a conscientious mechanic will conduct a road test before returning your car after carrying out major repairs, you should upload the entire site to the server on which it will be hosted and test it in detail as if you were a visitor. If possible, carry out this test several times using various browsers and various platforms.

It is at this point that you may discover that certain images that displayed so well when you tested your site locally are replaced by the "image not found" icon. This is all too familiar to those who have prepared their site in Windows and then uploaded it to a UNIX server. The cause is simple: although Windows considers upper and lower case letters identical in filenames, UNIX does not.

The easiest way to avoid this type of problem is to systematically spell all filenames as lower case.

Examples of tests

Syntax with HTML Validator

We submitted an HTML document to this checker whose display

in Netscape and Internet Explorer did not seem to cause any
problems. This did not stop HTML Validator from giving a list of
23 errors. The main ones are given below.

....

```
CSE 3310 HTML Validator v2.00B (Unregistered)
```

[...]

....

```
 1: <HTML>
 2: <HEAD>
 3: <TITLE>The Gnome & Rh&ocirc;ne Motorcycle
    Club</TITLE>
```

Error number 1 in line 3:
The character entity "& Rhô" was not
found in the HTML Configuration.

[...]

```
12: <NOFRAMES>
```

Error number 2 for tag beginning in line 12:
The tag name "NOFRAMES" must be closed but the
closing tag was not found.

[...]

```
58: <IMG SRC="x_cata.gif" ALT="Catalogue GR
    1929"border=0></A>
59: <IMG SRC="x_autre.gif" ALT=" " border=0></
    A>
```

Error number 6 for tag beginning in line 59:
The closing tag for "A" was found, but the tag
was never opened or has been closed too many
times.

[...]

Error number 8 in line 62:
A quotation mark was found that is not within a tag.
The character entity " should be used instead of the quotation character.

[...]

```
66: </TABLE>
67: </TABLE>
```

Error number 9 for tag beginning in line 67:
The closing tag for "TABLE" was found, but it should have been preceded by the closing tag for "TD" which was opened in line 21 (nesting error).

```
68: <HR>
69:
70: <CENTER><TABLE BORDER=0>
71: <TR><TD><CENTER><FONT SIZE=-2><I>This site
is    better viewed with<BR><IMG
SRC="now8.gif" ALIGN=middle> or
<IMG SRC="ie_anima.gif" ALIGN=middle></I></
  FONT></   TD></TR>
```

Error number 11 for tag beginning in line 71:
The attribute value "-2" for the attribute "SIZE" was not enclosed in double quotation marks when it must be.

[...]

```
76: <IMG SRC="/cgi-bin
  counter?mdreyfus&font=stencil&width=3">
persons have already visited this site.
```

Error number 17 in line 76:
High ASCII characters found. HTML documents should not contain ASCII characters with ASCII values greater than 127.

[...]

```
95: </HTML>
Error number 23 for tag beginning in line 95:
The closing tag for "HTML" was found, but it
should have been preceded by the closing tag
for "NOFRAMES" which was opened in line 12
(nesting error).
```

Certain errors do not cause problems (forgetting double quotation marks around -2 in line 71, for example, or the direct use of the quotation marks instead of the entity " in line 62), but others are more serious, such as the presence of a </A> end tag in line 59 (which might indicate that you forgot to open one higher up) or the direct use of the character "&" (which could mislead some browsers).

▇▇▇▇ Checking services

In addition to the checking tools that we have briefly looked at, there are some checking services that you can use over long distance. You connect to their server (a Web site like any other) and you give the URL of the site to test. It will send you back a list of the errors found. In this instance, you combine the three phrases that we have examined, although it takes longer to verify as the checker has to download all your pages and all your images to do its work.

These checking tools are often made up of scripts written in PERL or a similar language. We have tried three whose URLs you will find in Chapter 12 and whose results are not encouraging. In addition to the waiting time, some have remained with the old versions of HTML (2.0 or 3.0). It is not as easy to configure these as with tools you have downloaded. Only one gave something like a satisfactory result, WWWeblint whose services are charged for (but free for HTML documents with fewer than 2,048 characters).

Chapter 5

Lists, pictures and multimedia

The contents for this chapter

- Creating lists
- Inserting pictures
- Using sounds
- Displaying animations

To display a number of items or a list of objects, subjects or facts, you might be happy with ordinary paragraphs. There are also magazines and newspapers (and not always the minor ones) which use pictures sparingly. But if the Web had had to limit itself to such meagreness, it would most certainly have never gained the popularity it has today.

In this chapter we will finish with text by studying lists and then examine the means that HTML offers to enhance the presentation of text with pictures, sounds and animation.

CREATING LISTS

Although HTML officially recognises five types of lists, only three of these are actually used. We will leave the other two well alone (menu lists and directory lists). As the name suggests, this type of formating is used to present collections of related objects in a way that makes them stand out from paragraphs of ordinary text.

What these lists have in common is that they are contained in a list container tag inside which each item is preceded by a special markup command.

Lists are often used to make up navigation menus. We will see them performing this role in Chapter 6.

■■■■ Bullet pointed lists

These are also called unordered lists and they are displayed as a slightly indented paragraph preceded by a "bullet point", i.e. a typographical sign which is usually a large black dot. They are used to set out a group of objects when the order in which they are listed is not important: for example, a list of the works of a writer or the names of flowers that you have planted in your garden. The container tag for bullet-pointed lists is `<UL> ... </UL>` (*unordered list*). Each item must be preceded by the empty tag `<LI>` (see Figure 5.1).

```
<HTML>
<HEAD>
<TITLE>Bullet pointed lists</TITLE>
</HEAD>
```

```
<BODY>
<H2>My flower garden</H2>
In my garden there are many colourful flowers:
<UL>
<LI>Red dahlias and yellow dahlias
<LI>Yellow irises and blue irises
<LI>Purple pansies and white pansies
<LI>Cosmoses of all colours
</UL>
And all these colours follow the seasons.
</BODY>
</HTML>
```

Figure 5.1: A simple bullet-pointed list

The TYPE= attribute allows you to choose between three types of point, but you can do better if you want to enhance the display of the list as we shall see below with regard to images.

Ordered lists

This type of list is used to number a series of consecutive objects (the months of the year, for example) or to describe the exact order of operations to be carried out (such as installing a software program). Their presentation resembles that of a bullet-pointed list in this regard except that the points are replaced by numbers in

ascending order. The container tag for an ordered list is <OL>...
</OL> (*ordered list*). Each item must be preceded by the empty
tag <LI>. Here is an example of an ordered list, the result of which
you can see in Figure 5.2.

```
<HTML>
<HEAD>
<TITLE>Ordered list</TITLE>
</HEAD>
<BODY>
<H2>Installing software</H2>
<OL>
<LI>Decompress the ZIP file.
<LI>Execute the program SETUP.EXE.
<LI>Choose the installation directory.
<LI>Answer the questions asked by the dialog
box.
</LI>
</BODY>
</HTML>
```

Figure 5.2: Example of an ordered list

You can change the type of numbering of the items (Arabic
numbers, Roman numbers, letters, etc.) and change the starting
value by using the attributes TYPE= and START=.

Definition list

This type of list is used when you want to list coupled items, i.e. a term and its definition, a chapter and its contents, or simply to construct a glossary. Constructing these lists is a little different from the two previous lists. Here, the container tag is called <DL> ... </DL> (*definition list*). Each term is preceded by the markup tag <DT> and each definition by the markup tag <DD>. Figure 5.3 shows how the following example will be displayed:

```
<HTML>
<HEAD>
<TITLE>Definition list</TITLE>
</HEAD>
<BODY>
<H2>A few quotes</H2>
<DL>
<DT>Flowers
   <DD>It is a strange evening when flowers
have souls. <I>(Albert Samain)</I>
<DT>Justice
   <DD>Unable to strengthen justice, force was
justified. <I>(Blaise Pascal)</I>
<DT>Mirrors
   <DD>Mirrors would do well reflecting before
sending back images. <I>(Jean Cocteau)</I>
<DT>Natural
   <DD>Chase what's natural, it will come back
galloping. <I>(Destouches)</I>
<DT>Work
   <DD>I love work, it fascinates me and I can
stay seated for hours thinking about it.
<I>(Jerome K. Jerome)</I>
</BODY>
</HTML>
```

The indentation of the markup commands is only used here to aid reading the text.

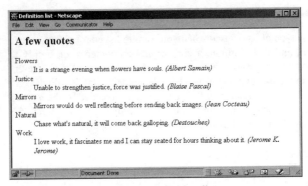

Figure 5.3: An example of a definition list

Nested lists

Most HTML container tags may be nested one inside another. List
container tags are no exception to this rule. By mixing styles of
bullet-pointed lists and ordered lists, you can achieve an attractive
display as illustrated in the following example, which is displayed
as shown in Figure 5.4:

```
<HTML>
<HEAD>
<TITLE>Nested lists</TITLE>
</HEAD>
<BODY>
<H2>Calendar of first term's activities</H2>
<OL>
  <LI>January
  <UL>
    <LI>Visit to the National Gallery.
    <LI>Concert at the Albert Hall (Debussy).
  </UL>
  <LI>February
  <UL>
    <LI>Excursion to Nice.
    <LI><I>Holiday on Ice</I> in London.
    <LI>Visit to the Natural History Museum.
```

```
  </UL>
  <LI>March
  <UL>
    <LI>Visit to the Transport Museum.
    <LI>Concert at the Barbican (Mozart and
Bach).
  </UL>
</OL>
Reservations should be made in the usual way.
</BODY>
</HTML>
```

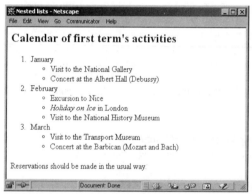

Figure 5.4: Example of nested lists

INSERTING PICTURES

Among the many existing image formats, HTML currently recognises two: GIF and JPEG. A third format, PNG, should slowly replace GIF for reasons associated with the dark history of copyright. However, to date it has only been partially implemented, as much in browsers as in editors or image converters.

What these formats have in common is that they offer a large degree of compression, but at the cost of losing a certain amount of information (and hence a loss of quality) in the case of JPEG images. GIF images are limited to 256 colours, but this is not too much of a problem, because this corresponds to the number of colours most used on the Web.

Generally, and without going into long explanations, you should use the JPEG format for photographs which include a lot of detail and reserve GIF for drawings and schematic diagrams created with a drawing program.

In addition to Web and ftp sites where you can find images (but beware of using copyrighted material) there is a fairly new and practical way of creating them – digital cameras – which create images ready to be inserted into a page. For around £200 to £300 you can currently find models of sufficient quality (size of images 640 × 480) quite suited for illustrating an HTML document. Images produced may be used as they are or after editing (cropping or adjustments in lighting, contrast or colour balance) using graphical software.

In Chapter 12 you will find a list of Web sites from which you will be able to download images.

■■■ The *<IMG>* container tag

To insert an image, you use the `<IMG>` ... `</IMG>` container tag, which includes the indispensable `SRC=` attribute which points to the name of the image possibly preceded by its file path. Here is a simple example using an image. The result is displayed in Figure 5.5.

```
<HTML>
<HEAD>
<TITLE>A simple image</TITLE>
</HEAD>
<BODY>
<DIV ALIGN=CENTER>
<IMG SRC="knight.gif">
```

```
<H2>The time of the crusades</H2>
</DIV>
My lords, it would be better for the storyteller
who only wishes to please to avoid long tales.
The subject matter of this tale is so lovely
and so various, what use would it be to lengthen
it? I will therefore briefly describe how,
after a very long time, having wandered by sea
and land, Rohalt the Faithful came to Cornwall.
<HR WIDTH=60%>
</BODY>
</HTML>
```

Figure 5.5: Example of the use of an image

The *ALIGN* attribute

The <IMG> container tag may include another attribute, ALIGN=, which allows you to achieve the effect of wrapping the picture in text (see Figure 5.6, which was obtained from the following HTML document):

```
<HTML>
<HEAD>
<TITLE>The ABC Motorcycle (1924)</TITLE>
```

```
</HEAD>
<BODY>
<H2 ALIGN=CENTER>The ABC Motorcycle (1924)</
H2>
<IMG SRC="abcd.gif" ALIGN=right>
Based on the 398 cc engine of the <I>All British
(Engine) Company</I>, this motorcycle had a
large number of technical innovations. It had
overhead valves and a four speed gearbox.
Transmission is achieved by a chain and the
frame was suspended. The flat cylinder
arrangement was very rare for that time.
<BR>
It does not seem that this search for innovation
brought rewards. Eventually, we know how
successfully BMW took up this arrangement which
continues to be sold in 1997.
<HR>
</BODY>
</HTML>
```

Figure 5.6: The effect obtained by wrapping text around an image

The ALIGN= *attribute may take other values allowing the image to be aligned horizontally or vertically with the text that surrounds it.*

The *ALT* attribute

Downloading an image may take quite a bit of time. This is why some surfers deactivate image downloads (Options/Auto Download of images in Netscape Navigator). So that they are not completely deprived of information, HTML offers the ALT= attribute which allows you to substitute text chosen by the author for an image. In the previous example, if you replace

```
<IMG SRC="abcd.gif" ALIGN=right>
```
by
```
<IMG SRC="abcd.gif" ALIGN=right ALT="Photo of
the ABC Motorcycle">
```

and you download the document in a browser where downloading of images has been deactivated, you obtain the result shown in Figure 5.7.

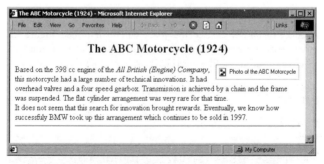

Figure 5.7: With the ALT attribute you have part of the information conveyed by an image which is not displayed

The *WIDTH* and *HEIGHT* attributes

These attributes allow the *display* size of an image to be specified. The time for downloading an image will not be changed, but its display will take a little more time because calculations must be made to change its size.

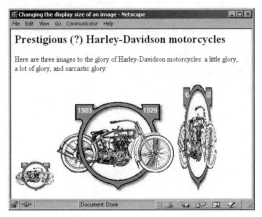

Figure 5.8: Changing the display size of an image

If the ratio of reduction is not the same in both dimensions, it will produce *anamorphosis*, i.e. the image will be deformed. Figure 5.8 gives two examples, one with and one without deformation, obtained from the following HTML text:

```
<HTML>
<HEAD>
<TITLE>Changing the display size of an image</
TITLE>
</HEAD>
<BODY>
<H2>Prestigious (?) Harley-Davidson motorcycles
</H2>
Here are three images to the glory of Harley-
Davidson motorcycles: a little glory, a lot
of glory and sarcastic glory:
```

```
<P>
<IMG SRC="harley.gif" WIDTH=86 HEIGHT=62>
<IMG SRC="harley.gif">
<IMG SRC="harley.gif" WIDTH=86 HEIGHT=225>
</BODY>
</HTML>
```

 It is not advisable to use this method to enlarge an image, because it might cause the disagreeable "staircase" effect.

Transparent images

In Figure 5.5, our knight from the crusades was perfectly separate from the white background of the screen because he was drawn on a background of this colour. However, let's suppose that we chose wallpaper for the background of our image using the command:

```
<BODY BACKGROUND="fond.gif">
```

Figure 5.9 shows what we would have obtained.

Figure 5.9: On a coloured background, the background of the image is clearly shown

Type 89a GIF images have an interesting property: transparency. You choose a colour (the background colour of the image) and with the aid of a graphical editor (the excellent LViewPro, for example) you choose the background colour, which should be transparent, and save the image. Figure 5.10 shows the result obtained with our previous example.

To give a tidy impression it is important that the background of the image is uniform.

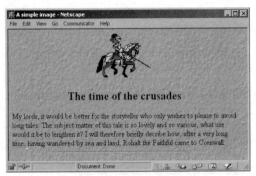

Figure 5.10: With a transparent background the image is correctly displayed

Using big images

In the two preceding examples (the crusades and ABC motorcycles), the sizes of the images were 3,493 and 28,851 bytes respectively, which would translate to an average download time at 28,800 bps of 2 seconds for the first and 11 seconds for the second. That is reasonable and does not risk testing the patience of the visitor. However, to use a large image occupying almost the whole surface of the screen, this could take more than a minute. The following example (see Figure 5.11) invites you, by clicking on a small image (a *thumbnail*) of 99 × 75 pixels (8,575 bytes), to download the enlarged image of 413 × 314 pixels (119,138 bytes). For this, you use the link container tags <A> ... </A> that we will study in Chapter 6.

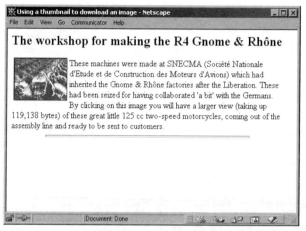

Figure 5.11: Using a thumbnail to suggest downloading the enlarged image

It is a good idea to tell visitors the size of the image to be downloaded so they can make an informed decision.

```
<HTML>
<HEAD>
<TITLE>Using a thumbnail to download an image
</TITLE>
</HEAD>
<BODY>
<H2>The workshop for making the R4 Gnome &amp;
Rh&ocirc;ne</H2>
<A HREF="atelier2.gif"><IMG SRC="atelier1.gif"
ALIGN=LEFT></A>
These machines were made at SNECMA
(Soci&eacute;t&eacute; Nationale d'Etude et
de Construction des Moteurs d'Avions) which
had inherited the Gnome &amp; Rh&ocirc;ne
factories after the Liberation. These had been
seized for having collaborated 'a bit' with
```

```
the Germans. By clicking on this image you
will have a larger view (taking up 119,138
bytes) of these great little 125 cc two-speed
motorcycles, coming out of the assembly line
and ready to be sent to customers.
<HR WIDTH=75% SIZE=3>
</BODY>
</HTML>
```

Figure 5.12 shows the enlarged image which would have taken more than 40 seconds to download at 28,800 bps. To get back to the previous page the visitor should click on the "previous page" command in their browser.

Figure 5.12: The picture at its full size

Some sites which allow you to download images (most of the time free of any copyright, although you should check) offer a catalogue similar to the one shown in Figure 5.13 while explaining that if you click on the thumbnail you will open a new window in which the full-size image will be displayed to make your choice easier.

Figure 5.13: A catalogue of images to download presented as thumbnails

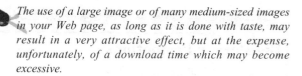

The use of a large image or of many medium-sized images in your Web page, as long as it is done with taste, may result in a very attractive effect, but at the expense, unfortunately, of a download time which may become excessive.

Using images in a list

For a more attractive bullet-pointed list, you can use images disguised as bullet points. But you can no longer use the `<UL>` ... `</UL>` container tag. The trick is to achieve the usual indentation by using the definition list inside which you only use the `<DD>` tag. Here is an example, illustrated in Figure 5.14.

```
<HTML>
<HEAD>
<TITLE>More attractive lists</TITLE>
</HEAD>
<H1>Big Bazaar Promotions</H1>
```

```
This week we offer you especially the following
articles:
<DL>
<DD><IMG SRC="cle.gif"> Universal security key.
<DD><IMG SRC="mae.gif"> A steam-powered type
writer.
<DD><IMG SRC="pendule.gif"> A grandfather clock
powered by a diesel engine.
<DD><IMG SRC="telefone.gif"> A gas-powered
telephone.
</DL>
<HR NOSHADE>
</BODY>
</HTML>
```

More easily, you can use identically coloured images in the form
of a small geometric shape (ball, circle, square, etc) to replace the
bullet point in this type of list.

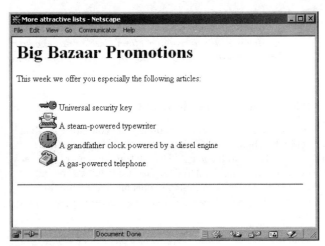

Figure 5.14: An attractively–presented list

USING SOUNDS

Like pictures, sound files (also called *audio files*) exist in many formats. However, an image is static and once downloaded you see it all at once, whereas sounds requires the element of *time* to be heard. Most audio files are digital sound files which the element generally means that, apart from very short sounds, they are larger than image files. We must, however, mention MIDI files, which only contain commands for synthesisers and can only therefore reproduce music and no spoken words or natural sounds.

Browsers are rarely able to directly interpret the audio files they receive. For that, they must have recourse to helper programs called *plug-ins*. When a browser receives an audio file, it knows what type it is by looking at its extension. It then consults the list of plug-ins that have been installed. If it finds the right one, it may initiate sound reproduction once the whole file has been downloaded.

There is a system of transferring audio files called RealAudio which, with the aid of very efficient compression algorithms and very clever use of buffers on receipt of a file, allows an audio file to be reproduced before it has been completely transferred. This, however, requires special servers which are not generally made available by Internet access providers to non-business customers.
Don't be upset! The sound quality is most often poor, reproduction suffering from the affects of dynamic routing in the Internet, and these files are only really suitable for sounds or voice.

<BGSOUND> markup command

This is the easiest way to reproduce an audio file. Unfortunately, although it is recognised by Internet Explorer (which is what you'd expect since it was created by Microsoft), Netscape ignores it completely. Its syntax is very simple because it only includes two attributes: SRC= to indicate the name of the audio file and LOOP=

to indicate the number of repetitions to be carried out (the values "INFINITE" and 0 mean "continuously"). For example:

```
<BGSOUND SRC="cleopha.mid" LOOP=2>
```

Once the file is loaded, you will hear Scott Joplin's ragtime tune Cleopha twice in a row.

Links to audio files

Here, we will jump ahead a little and take a look at something to be covered in the next chapter and remember an earlier tip. The "traditional" way of reproducing an audio file consists of creating a link to that file. However, unlike an image file, the contents of the screen remain and a small auxiliary window appears containing a few controls which allow the reproduction to be stopped at a given moment or to move to another place in the file. The following HTML document acts as a small jukebox (see Figure 5.15).

```
<HTML>
<HEAD>
<TITLE>A few sounds</TITLE>
</HEAD>
<BODY>
<H1>Jukebox</H1>
Here are a few ragtime tunes from Scott Joplin.
Click on the one you want to listen to:
<UL>
<LI><A HREF="cleopha.mid">Cleopha</A> (15 Kb)
<LI><A HREF="kitten.mid">Kitten on the keys</A>
(17 Kb)
<LI><A HREF="entertnr.mid">The entertainer</A>
(19 Kb)
<LI><A HREF="micicipi.mid">Mississippi rag</A>
(16 Kb)
<LI><A HREF="mapple.mid">Mapple life rag</A> (20
Kb)
</UL>
<HR>
</HTML>
```

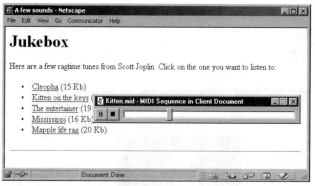

Figure 5.15: A small HTML jukebox

As with images, it is a good idea to tell your visitor the size of the audio file so that they can make an informed decision.

DISPLAYING ANIMATIONS

There are many ways of displaying something that moves on the screen. We will briefly describe three of those most used.

Traditional animations

Three formats come to the fore: AVI, MPEG (again!) and QuickTime, created by Apple and very popular. Here, we will not discuss their respective features. In each case, the navigator must have the appropriate plug-in (or helper). Luckily, there is a version of QuickTime for Windows. The display window is a long way from occupying the entire screen (see Figure 5.16). Its size is only 235 × 290 pixels and it runs for 25 seconds. The size of the file is 3.4 MB. Such a large file would fit easily on a CD-ROM, but you can understand that it would be better to find alternative solutions to transfer these animations over the Internet.

Transferring animation files on the Internet is only for those who have a heavy-duty direct connection. As you cannot know whether your visitor has such a connection, it is recommended that you make downloading optional rather than imposing it on them.

Figure 5.16: Display of an AVI file

Animated GIFs

There is a much more economical solution if you are happy with a few basic movements. This technology, called "animated GIFs", is derived from animated drawings. You prepare a series of drawings (from 5 to 10 or more, depending on the complexity of the movement to be reproduced) and load them into a special image editor (GIFANIM or Paintshop Pro's GIF animator, for example) which will assemble them. Once this file (which has a GIF extension like a fixed image file) is completely downloaded, the browser quickly loads the images one after another, so giving the illusion of movement. This technique, which only requires reasonably–sized images, is often used, particularly for the banner advertisements showing sponsorship which are becoming more and more common on commercial Web sites (and also on some private pages).

Shockwave

Created by the developer Macromedia, Shockwave is a tool for the interpretation of elaborate "scenes" using that developer's editor Director. The necessary plug-in may be downloaded freely from the developer's site. The creator of a Web page must own the Director application and, once his animation is programmed, compress the file with a utility also supplied by Macromedia. He must then insert a link from his Web page to the file. Given the price of the application ($850 in the United States), its use is mainly reserved for business purposes.

VRML

This is a virtual reality modelling language. The Web author defines his virtual world symbolically using a tool called Live3D. A fairly small text file results which must be interpreted in the browser by the plug-in WebFX. You can think of VRML as a 3D extension to HTML and, in this regard, it would take a whole book three times larger than this one to teach you how to use it. If you are interested you can find a few references in Chapter 12.

Chapter 6

The very essence of the Web: links

THE CONTENTS FOR THIS CHAPTER

- The principle of links
- Three types of link
- More about links

In previous chapters, we have been examining a single page, mentioning links only in passing and without elaborating on exactly how they allow you to move from one page to another or from one type of file to another. With the knowledge that we have now acquired, it is time to deal with them more fully. This will be our aim in Chapter 6.

THE PRINCIPLE OF LINKS

The Web is often described as a huge library full of all the works published across the world. Of course, in real life such a library would be impossible. It is possible, however, virtually, so that we can potentially refer to any work, wherever it is stored, without moving from our homes. This is the very essence of the Web.

From any page of a site, you can find *links* which point to other pages in the same site or to other sites, wherever they may be. Specifically, these links are *addresses* which are called URLs. However, what is interesting for the visitor is not the address itself, but what can be found there, and so generally the address is not displayed. Instead, what you can find there is highlighted in the text (by underlining it and displaying it in another colour, often blue). The following HTML text contains the three usual forms of link, as illustrated in Figure 6.1.

A URL (Uniform Resource Locator) is the address of a resource on the Internet (not necessarily the Web).

```
<HTML>
<HEAD>
<TITLE>A basic anchor</TITLE>
</HEAD>
<BODY>
<H1>The last works of Mozart</H1>
The last three years of the life of Mozart
were to be his most creative. <A
HREF="cosi.htm">
Cosi fan tutte</A> was written in Vienna in
1790. <A HREF="http://www.mozarteum.de/
zauberflote.html"> The magic flute</A> was
performed in September 1791. The <A
HREF="#Requiem">Requiem</A> was to be Mozart's
last work. He died on the 5th December 1791.
<HR>
</BODY>
</HTML>
```

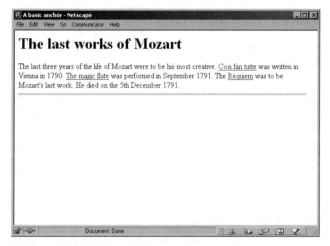

Figure 6.1: How links are presented

If the visitor were to click on one of the words in the underlined group "The Magic Flute", the browser would load the file **zauberflote.html** which is located on the Web server **http:// www.mozarteum.de** (note: this is a fictitious site!). The contents of this HTML document would replace what is currently displayed on the screen.

Avoid using accented characters or characters which have a special meaning (colon, space, dollar sign, for example) in a URL because you have to enter these with an escape sequence different from character entities (a "%" character followed by the hexadecimal ASCII code of the character you want to display).

THREE TYPES OF LINK

In our example, we saw three types of link. However, they have the same basic structure:

```
<A HREF="name_of_resource">text of the anchor</A>
```

The HREF attribute means *Hypertext Reference*. It is generally followed by the URL of the file to be loaded, which corresponds to the source (Web server, FTP server, mail server, or simply a local document) whatever it might be and assuming that you have the necessary plug-in. You may also find a pointer to another section of the same file if you simply want to display another part of the HTML file that has already been loaded.

▬▬▬ External links

If you want to load a page located on another server, the URL starts with the name of the server. If you want to access a page other than the home page, this server name will be followed by the name of the file to be loaded, which itself is probably followed by the pathway. The URL starts with the name of the protocol. For a Web file, it is **http://**. For an FTP server, it would be **ftp://**. We will return to this point later. For the moment, let's start with Web files.

*When no file name follows the server name, a default HTML file is loaded. Its name is generally **index.htm, index.html, default.htm** or **default.html**.*

The file that you will load is of little importance. For everything to work well, it is enough that the server and the file exist at the places mentioned. And, of course, that the Internet link works. This is the most general (and most wide-spread) form of *external link*. This is how you reference other sites and this is why you may hear talk of a worldwide spider's web. In our example, this type is represented by:

```
<A HREF="http://www.mozarteum.de/
zauberflote.html">
The Magic Flute</A>
```

Here, the question of *relative links* and *absolute links,* which we will discuss later, does not arise: references are, by necessity, absolute.

Internal links

These *internal links* are links to pages situated on the same computer as the server. Be careful though, this is not your personal hard disk but that of the service provider who is hosting your site. These pages may or may not be in the same directory and this poses the problem of relative and absolute links. In our example, this type is represented by:

```
<A HREF="cosi.htm">Cosi fan tutte</A>
```

A directory is one of the elements of the branch structure of a hard disk. You can also use the word folder (especially on a Macintosh).

Moving around the same file

If your page is long and it seems illogical to sub-divide it into short pages of less than five screens (an analysis of *the Magic Flute* and its masonic references, for example), it would be helpful for your reader to have a means of navigating around it. For this, using our example, you could sub-divide the analysis into several sections all situated in the same HTML document:

- "Circumstances of composition";

- "Mozart and freemasonry";

- "A thematic analysis of the work";

- "A philosophical analysis of the work";

- "Circumstances surrounding its first performance";

- "Reception by the public", etc.

Your visitor won't necessarily read everything from start to finish, preferring instead to read the sections in an order which is not the same as the one you provided. To help the reader, you can place markers in front of each of the sections (which will, of course, be preceded by a sub-title – a level 2 or 3 sub-title, for example – to make the doument more user-friendly). These markers are called *anchors* and their syntax takes the form:

```
<A NAME="reference">
```

This form corresponds to the link:

```
<A HREF="#Requiem">Requiem</A>
```

The hash sign (#) may only appear in the link itself. It is a very common fault to include it in the anchor definition, which results in the link not working.

Another important point: here upper and lower case letters are different. `<A NAME="requiem">` *would not allow a link to be formed. You have to write* `<A NAME="Requiem">`.

MORE ABOUT LINKS

Given their importance, we will emphasise a few aspects of using links. Remember, however, that this book is not a course in HTML. Chapter 12 contains a list of bibliographic and other references which would allow any interested reader to find out more about the subjects covered here.

Relative links and absolute links

For various reasons, you might change your access provider or simply your host site (which is often the same). You would then need to transport your entire site to a new host.

*Do not forget to keep an exact and entire copy of your site on your hard disk **and**, of course, on another medium (diskette, cassette, removable hard disk, etc.)*

Let's say that you are an orderly (even obsessive) person and that you have decided to create the directory structure shown in Figure 6.2. Your home page (see Figure 6.3) could be presented like this:

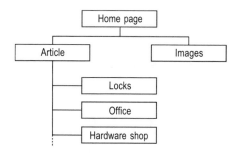

Figure 6.2: So everything is tidy, you have created a meticulous directory structure

```
<HTML>
<HEAD>
<TITLE>Some more attractive lists</TITLE>
</H>Big Bazaar Promotions</H1>
This week we offer you especially the following
articles:
<DL>
<DD><IMG  SRC="images/cle.gif">
    <A  HREF="http://www.monserveur.fr/dupont/
bazar/articles/serrures/cle.html"> Universal
security key.
    </A>
<DD><IMG  SRC="images/mae.gif">
    <A  HREF="http://www.monserveur.fr/dupont/
bazar/articles/bureau/mae.htm">A steam-powered
typewriter.
```

```
    </A>
<DD><IMG  SRC="images/pendule.gif">
    <A  HREF="http://www.monserveur.fr/dupont/
bazar/articles/bureau/pendule.htm">  A
grandfather clock powered by a diesel engine.
    </A>
<DD><IMG  SRC="images/telefone.gif">
    <A  HREF="http://www.monserveur.fr/dupont/
bazar/bureau/bureau/phone.htm"> A gas-powered
telephone.
    </A>
</DL>
<P>
By clicking on any article you find interesting,
you can find out more about it (such as its
description and price, etc.)
</P>
<HR NOSHADE>
</BODY>
</HTML>
```

Note how the indentations (which will not be seen in the browser window) make reading the document easier.

Figure 6.3: Four links in your presentation

Here, you could have relative references for images and absolute references for documents, but doing it this way is clumsy, because if you change your host site, or if your host, carrying out a reorganisation, gives you a new directory with another name (without asking you), you will have to change all the internal references scattered throughout your site. It would have been better to content yourself with internal references and write, for example:

```
<DD><IMG SRC="images/pendule.gif">
    <A HREF="articles/bureau/pendule.htm">
    A grandfather clock powered by a diesel engine.
    </A>
```

By default, it is the **http://** protocol that is taken into account and the file will be searched for in the current directory which is the home page's directory. This type of internal link is therefore a *relative* reference. If your main directory (the home page's directory) is changed, all you will have to do is create the same directory structure and you won't have to change anything inside your documents.

There is also the <BASE> markup command which allows a reference directory other than that of the home page to be specified. Its use is mainly reserved for special cases.

Using images as links

Up until now, we decided that our links would be carried out from text. However, nothing stops you linking from an image. This is often more clear. To enclose the links with a coloured frame (see Figure 6.4), which is blue in Windows by default, it is enough to change each of the references in the following way (for the first reference, for example):

```
<DD>
  <A HREF="/bazar/articles/serrures/cle.html">
    <IMG SRC="images/cle.gif">
  </A>
  Universal security key.
```

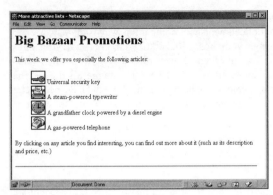

Figure 6.4: Using images for links

There are cases when the image is itself enough, as in the following example, which has been suggested for musicians and which offers material on the '3Bs' (Bach, Beethoven and Brahms). The portraits of these musicians are easily recognisable and any text would be pointless.

```
<HTML>
<HEAD>
  <!- - Created with AOLpress/2.0 - ->
  <TITLE>The 3 Bs</TITLE>
</HEAD>
<BODY>
<DIV ALIGN=Center>
<A HREF="bach.htm">     <IMG SRC="bach.gif"
    ALT="Jean-Sebastien Bach"></A>
<A HREF="bethoven.htm"><IMG SRC="bethoven.gif"
    ALT="Ludwig van Beethoven"></A>
<A HREF="brahms.htm">   <IMG SRC="brahms.gif"
    ALT="Johannes Brahms"></A>
<FONT FACE="Elfring-elite" SIZE="7">
<H1>Les 3 B</H1>
<P>
  <HR>
<P>
</BODY>
</HTML>
```

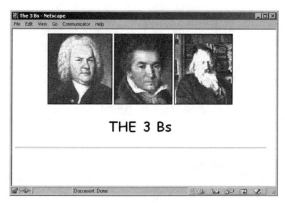

Figure 6.5: For a subject like this, the images speak for themselves and no text is needed

Links to other objects

We have met two types: links to images (using a thumbnail) and links to an audio file. However, there are many others, especially to other Internet resources: file servers (FTP) or news servers, for example. A special case is one you will almost always find at the end of a site, where the author invites the visitor to offer an opinion. There is the special `<ADDRESS>` container tag, created mainly to give your contact details and e-mail address. However, this is really a relic from the past, because it is restricted to displaying the text it contains in italics. That it why we suggest that you forget it.

Here is how you may end your Web site:

```
[...]
<BR>
<HR>
This page was written by Arthur Pond whom you
can contact at <A HREF="mailto:
arthur.pond@myserver.co.uk">arthur.pond@myserver.co.
uk</A>.
<P>
```

```
<IMG SRC="stones.gif">
</BODY>
</HTML>
```

Figure 6.6 shows how this is displayed. You will note the special form of the **mailto:** protocol which does not include a slash. Repeating the e-mail address is justified because it tells the visitor that if he clicks on the address an e-mail application will be launched (both Netscape Navigator and Internet Explorer have this function).

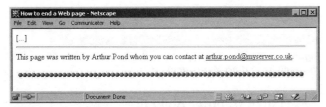

Figure 6.6: A traditional way to end a Web page

Rather than the traditional horizonatal rule, you could use graphical separation bars which are often coloured and often have a drawing at one end (a nest, a pair of scissors, a fish, an owl, etc.)

Chapter 7

Tables for everything

THE CONTENTS FOR THIS CHAPTER

- Creating and improving tables
- Working with cells
- Creating a links menu
- Using newspaper format
- Tables and HTML editors

The first versions of HTML did not allow sophisticated layouts and, in particular, the notion of a *table* in the sense used in word processing did not exist. Now that this gap has been filled, when you see what can be done with the `<TABLE>` ... `</TABLE>` tag, you wonder how we ever managed without them.

HTML 4.0 includes a number of new tags for tables which are only of marginal interest and which we will not discuss here. This is for two reasons: firstly, their usefulness is not obvious and, secondly, neither Netscape nor Microsoft appear to have shown any great enthusiasm to implement them. In any case, even if we limit ourselves to HTML 3.2, we will have enough tools to do pretty much anything we want.

CREATING AND IMPROVING TABLES

The whole of a table is defined inside the `<TABLE>` container tags in which you define the table row by row using a series of `<TR>`(*table row*) container tags. In each row, the cells are defined individually in `<TD>` (*table data*) container tags. Numerous attributes allow a great variety of layouts in this elementary structure.

We will start with a basic table without any embellishments. Figure 7.1 shows how Netscape Navigator renders the following HTML document:

```
<HEAD>
<TITLE>The simplest of tables</TITLE>
</HEAD>
<BODY>
<DIV ALIGN=CENTER>
<H2>IT hardware sales</H2>
<TABLE BORDER=1>
  <TR>
 <TD></TD><TD>1995</TD><TD>1996</TD><TD>1997</TD>
  </TR>
  <TR>
    <TD>Computers</TD><TD>23</TD><TD>41</
TD><TD>123</TD>
  </TR>
  <TR>
```

```
   <TD>Printers</TD><TD>7</TD><TD>31</
TD><TD>98</TD>
   </TR>
   <TR>
     <TD>Scanners</TD><TD>-</TD><TD>2</
TD><TD>11</TD>
   </TR>
   <TR>
     <TD>Modems</TD><TD>12</TD><TD>24</
TD><TD>47</TD>
   </TR>
</TABLE>
</DIV>
</BODY>
</HTML>
```

Figure 7.1: The simplest of tables

> *The* BORDER= *attribute specifies the thickness of the
> borders of the table and cells. If it is absent, the table
> would not have any borders at all.*

You can't say that this is particularly successful. It's a table: it
contains rows and columns inside which the cells contain values.
But it could be so much better.

A few improvements

We will start by placing a title above the table using the `<CAPTION>` ... `</CAPTION>` container tags which accept the ALIGN= attribute to which we will assign the value TOP so that the title is displayed above the table. By assigning the value BOTTOM, the title would be displayed underneath it. While we are at it, we will display it in bold in a larger font.

Finally, to display the column titles, instead of `<TD>` we will use the container tags provided specifically for this purpose: `<TH>` ... `</TH>` (*table heading*) and we will make the table larger by using the WIDTH= attribute placed in `<TABLE>`. Figure 7.2 shows how our modified HTML document is displayed:

```
<TABLE BORDER=1 WIDTH=400>
    <CAPTION ALIGN=TOP><B><FONT SIZE=+1>For the
last three years</FONT></B></CAPTION>
  <TR>
  <TH></TH><TH>1995</TH><TH>1996</TH><TH>1997</TH>
  </TR>
  <TR>
    <TD>Computers</TD><TD>23</TD><TD>41</TD><TD>123</TD>
  </TR>
  <TR>
    <TD>Printers</TD><TD>7</TD><TD>31</TD><TD>98</TD>
  </TR>
  <TR>
    <TD>Scanners</TD><TD>-</TD><TD>2</TD><TD>11</TD>
  </TR>
  <TR>
    <TD>Modems</TD><TD>12</TD><TD>24</TD><TD>47</TD>
  </TR>
</TABLE>
```

You will notice that the `<TH>` ... `</TH>` container tags centre the contents of the cell which it defines and displays it in bold.

Figure 7.2: Our simple table has been improved

▬▬▬ What can be in a cell?

Practically anything: a number, text, an image ... or even another table. The ability to place images in a table allows layouts which cannot be done any other way. As long as you get rid of the table border, the effect achieved is quite remarkable (see Figure 7.3).

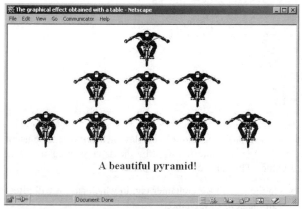

Figure 7.3: Pyramid obtained by a table without a border

```
<HTML>
<HEAD>
<TITLE>The graphical effect obtained with a
table</TITLE>
</HEAD>
<BODY>
<DIV ALIGN=CENTER>
<TABLE>
  <TR>
    <TD></TD>
    <TD></TD>
    <TD><IMG SRC="gnome.gif"></TD>
    <TD></TD>
    <TD></TD>
  </TR>
  <TR>
    <TD></TD>
    <TD><IMG SRC="gnome.gif"></TD>
    <TD><IMG SRC="gnome.gif"></TD>
    <TD><IMG SRC="gnome.gif"></TD>
  </TR>
  <TR>
    <TD><IMG SRC="gnome.gif"></TD>
    <TD><IMG SRC="gnome.gif"></TD>
    <TD><IMG SRC="gnome.gif"></TD>
    <TD><IMG SRC="gnome.gif"></TD>
    <TD><IMG SRC="gnome.gif"></TD>
  </TR>
</TABLE>
<H2>A beautiful pyramid!</H2>
</DIV>
</BODY>
</HTML>
```

You can use a different colour to display each cell of a table using the BGCOLOR= attribute followed by the name of a colour or an RGB value. This attribute may be placed:

- in the <TABLE> container tag, in which case it will affect all the cells of the table;

- in the <TR> container tag, in which case all the cells in a row are affected; or

- in the <TD> or <TH> container tags, in which case a single cell will be changed.

By combining these three properties, you can obtain special effects (see Figure 7.4 for the result obtained with Internet Explorer and Netscape Navigator). You will note that there are a few differences in interpretation.

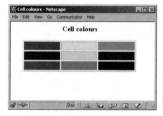 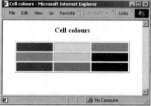

Netscape Navigator   Internet Explorer

Figure 7.4: Using a background colour for cell displays

Alignment of cell contents

The contents of a cell may be aligned in several ways using the attributes ALIGN= (horizontal alignment) and VALIGN= (vertical alignment) which may be placed in the container tags <TR>... </TR> (all the cells in a row will therefore be affected), <TD> ... </TD> or <TH> ... </TH> (a single cell only will be affected). In a row containing these alignments together, you will be able to specify the position of data in one or more cells. Here are the values that these attributes may take:

- ALIGN = LEFT, RIGHT or CENTER. The default value is = LEFT.

- VALIGN = TOP, BOTTOM, MIDDLE and BASELINE. The default value is = MIDDLE.

Returning to our example, we can improve it by adding
ALIGN=CENTER in each of the <TR> ... </TR> container
tags (except for those in the headings). Figure 7.5 shows the result
obtained.

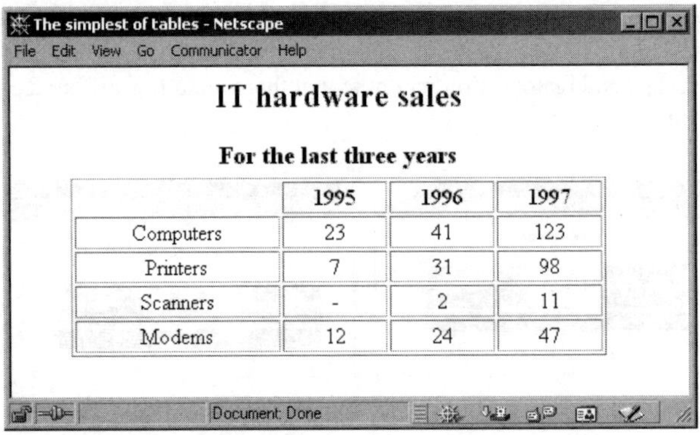

*Figure 7.5: The contents of the cells of our table is now
centred*

```
<TABLE BORDER=1 WIDTH=400>
<CAPTION ALIGN=TOP><B><FONT SIZE=+1>For the
last three years</FONT></B></CAPTION>
   <TR><TH></TH><TH>1995</TH><TH>1996</
TH><TH>1997</TH>
   </TR>
   <TR ALIGN=CENTER>
    <TD>Computers</TD><TD>23</TD><TD>41</
    TD><TD>123</TD>
   </TR>
   <TR ALIGN=CENTER>
    <TD>Printers</TD><TD>7</TD><TD>31</
TD><TD>98</TD>
   </TR>
   <TR ALIGN=CENTER>
     <TD>Scanners</TD><TD>-</TD><TD>2</
TD><TD>11</TD>
   </TR>
```

```
<TR ALIGN=CENTER>
    <TD>Modems</TD><TD>12</TD><TD>24</
TD><TD>47</TD>
</TR>
</TABLE>
```

WORKING WITH CELLS

A cell may be extended over its neighbour(s), towards the right
and/or downwards. The two attributes used for this purpose are
ROWSPAN=n for extending horizontally and COLSPAN=n for
extending vertically. You must take into account the fact that these
extensions "eat into" adjacent cells in the same or following rows
as shown in the example reproduced in Figure 7.6:

```
<HTML>
<HEAD>
<TITLE>Horizontal  and  Vertical  Extensions</
TITLE>
</HEAD>
<BODY>
<H2>A  table  with  cells  of  different  sizes</
H2>
<TABLE BORDER WIDTH=500>
<TR>
   <TD ALIGN=CENTER>ONE</TD>
   <TD ALIGN=CENTER COLSPAN=2>TWO</TD>
   <TD ALIGN=CENTER>THREE</TD>
   <TD ALIGN=CENTER>FOUR</TD>
</TR>
<TR>
   <TD ALIGN=CENTER>FIVE</TD>
   <TD ALIGN=CENTER>SIX</TD>
   <TD ALIGN=CENTER>SEVEN</TD>
   <TD ALIGN=CENTER ROWSPAN=3>EIGHT</TD>
   <TD ALIGN=CENTER>NINE</TD>
</TR>
<TR>
   <TD ALIGN=CENTER>TEN</TD>
   <TD ALIGN=CENTER>ELEVEN</TD>
```

```
   <TD ALIGN=CENTER>TWELVE</TD>
   <TD ALIGN=CENTER>THIRTEEN</TD>
</TR>
<TR>
   <TD ALIGN=CENTER>FOURTEEN</TD>
   <TD ALIGN=CENTER>FIFTEEN</TD>
   <TD ALIGN=CENTER>SIXTEEN</TD>
   <TD ALIGN=CENTER>SEVENTEEN</TD>
</TR>
</TABLE>
</BODY>
</HTML>
```

Horizontal and Vertical Extensions - Netscape

File Edit View Go Communicator Help

A table with cells of different sizes

ONE	TWO		THREE	FOUR
FIVE	SIX	SEVEN	EIGHT	NINE
TEN	ELEVEN	TWELVE		THIRTEEN
FOURTEEN	FIFTEEN	SIXTEEN		SEVENTEEN

Document: Done

Figure 7.6: Enlarging the cells of a table

The possibilities of alignment and enlargement can be shown using the following more complicated example, illustrated in Figures 7.7 and 7.8: firstly normal (without borders), then, to better show how the cells are grouped, with a border:

```
<HTML>
<HEAD>
   <TITLE>Extract from the list of prizes</
TITLE>
</HEAD>
<BODY>
<DIV ALIGN=CENTER>
<H2>EXTRACT FROM THE LIST OF PRIZES</H2>
<TABLE BORDER=1>
<TR><TD><B>Griffoutet Cost</B></TD>
    <TD>500 cc</TD><TD>1. </TD><TD>LANGLEY</TD>
```

```
</TR>
<TR><TD ROWSPAN=2><B>Six days in winter</B></TD>
     <TD>250 cc</TD><TD>1. ex-&aelig;quo</
TD><TD>LEVIN<BR>HARRIS</TD></TR>
     <TR><TD>500 cc</TD><TD>1. ex-&aelig;quo</
TD><TD>PARKER<BR>STEELE<BR>EDGSON</TD></TR>
</TR>
<TR><TD><B>Morlass Coast</B></TD>
     <TD>175 cc</TD><TD>1. </TD><TD>LANGLEY</TD>
</TR>
<TR><TD ROWSPAN=3><B>Paris-Nice</B></
TD><TD>175 cc</TD><TD>1. </TD><TD>LANGLEY</
TD></TR>
     <TR><TD>250 cc</TD><TD>1. ex-&aelig;quo</
TD><TD>LEVIN</TD></TR>
     <TR><TD>500 cc</TD><TD>1. ex-&aelig;quo</
TD><TD>NAPIER<BR>PARKER<BR>STEELE</TD></TR>
</TR>
<TR><TD ROWSPAN=3><B>Spring Circuit</B></
TD><TD>175 cc</TD><TD>1. </TD><TD>LANGLEY</
TD></TR>
     <TR><TD>250 cc</TD><TD>1. </
TD><TD>VICKERS</TD></TR>
     <TR><TD>500 cc</TD><TD>1. </
TD><TD>DEARING</TD></TR>
</TR>
<TR><TD><B>Ronchettes Circuit</B></TD>
     <TD>500 cc</TD><TD>1. </TD><TD>MARKS</
TD>
</TR>
<TR><TD ROWSPAN=2><B>Bordeaux-
Pyrenees<BR>Bordeaux</B></TD><TD>250 cc</
TD><TD>1. ex-&aelig;quo</TD><TD>LANGLEY</
TD></TR>
     <TR><TD>500 cc</TD><TD>1. ex-&aelig;quo</
TD><TD>HARRIS<BR>TATTERSALL<BR>MATHIAS<BR>COUNARD</
TD></TR>
</TR>
</TABLE>
</DIV>
</BODY>
</HTML>
```

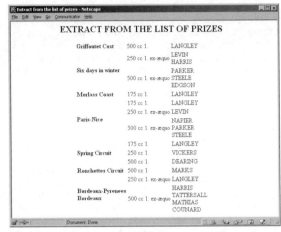

Figure 7.7: A complicated table

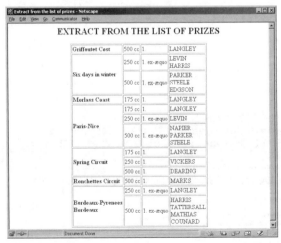

Figure 7.8: The same table with a border to show the structure of the cells

Some browsers have difficulty in properly displaying empty cells. If this happens, insert the character entity , which represents a non-breaking space, inside the cell. This should rectify the problem.

CREATING A LINKS MENU

The geometric layout of cells in a table allows a menu of links to be presented in a clear and consise way, provided you take care to use images as links and not text. The advantage of this method is that it makes the display independent of any options chosen by the visitor for his browser (such as font size). Figure 7.9 reproduces one of these menus. Here is an extract, including the first and last lines of the table (note the provision of an alternative text name for when the image cannot be displayed, using the ALT command):

```
<TABLE  BORDER=0  CELLPADDING=0  CELLSPACING=0>
 <TR>
  <TD><A HREF="histo1.htm">
    <IMG SRC="x_gr.gif" ALT="G&R" ></A></TD>
  <TD><A HREF="histo2.htm">
    <IMG SRC="x_amgr.gif" ALT="GRMC" ></A></
TD>
  <TD><A HREF="statuts.htm">
     <IMG SRC="x_statut.gif" ALT="Documents"
></A></TD>
  <TD><A HREF="services.htm">
    <IMG SRC="x_activi.gif" ALT="Activities>
    </A></TD>
  <TD><A HREF="refabri.htm">
    <IMG SRC="x_refab.gif"  ALT="Manufacture"
></A></TD>
 </TR>

[...]
```

```
<TR>
    <TD> </TD><TD  COLSPAN=3><A
HREF="ffve.htm">
    <IMG SRC="x_ffve.gif" ALT="Registration papers
    in the collection" ></A></TD>
  </TR>
</TABLE>
```

To juxtapose these images, two other attributes have been used, CELLPADDING *and* CELLSPACING*, which govern the space between the cells of a table.*

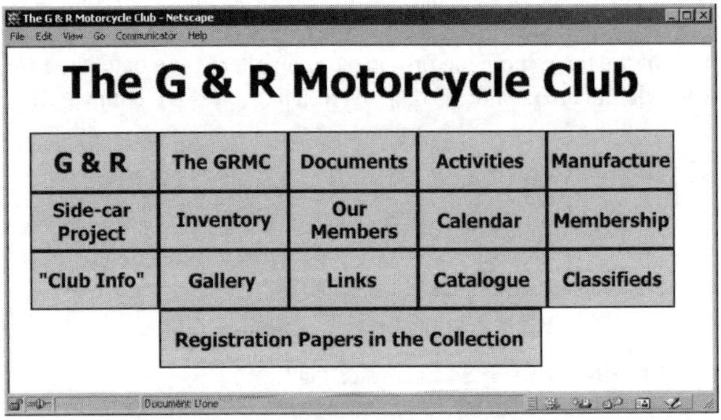

Figure 7.9: A links menu in the form of a table of images (the text alternative is displayed here)

You might have been quite happy placing <IMG> markup commands one after another separating every fourth one by a <BR> markup command. However, this way, when a visitor chooses a narrow screen size, the table alignments are retained and can be seen using the scrolling bars (see Figure 7.10) whereas, without a table, the images which comprise the links are displayed any old how (see Figure 7.11).

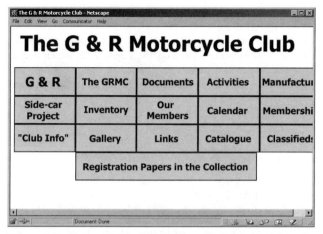

Figure 7.10: Using a table, the display of a links menu is not upset when the screen is too small

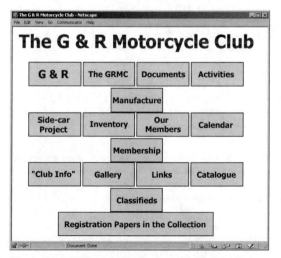

Figure 7.11: Without a table, the layout of the links menu muddled

USING NEWSPAPER FORMAT

To show the role that a table may play in the layout of a Web site, we will show how the page shown in Figure 7.12, which tries to copy the layout of a newspaper printed in three columns, was created. There isn't enough space to reproduce all the text. We will just extract the essence.

```
    [...]
<DIV ALIGN=CENTER>
<IMG SRC="fanta.gif">
<TABLE BORDER=0>
<TR VALIGN=top>

<TD WIDTH=185>
<FONT SIZE=6><B>The Chimpanzee</B></FONT>
<BR>
These are large monkeys without tails and
hairless faces, but it is our imagination alone
that has been able to suggest they are <I>
men of the forest</I>. Their stocky bodies,
short legs as compared to their arms, and
above all, elongated faces forming a type of
muzzle without a forehead when the animal is
an adult,
<BR><IMG SRC="monkey.gif"><BR>
imprint all the traits of their animal nature
on their outside. Only the young can offer any
remote similarity with the shapes of our
children. But
</TD>

<TD WIDTH=185>they have inspired us to make
comparisons of this type by a certain amount
of intelligence and by remarkable social
instincts. All these qualities

    [...]

<FONT SIZE=6><B>The Catoblepas</B></FONT>
<BR>
An extraordinary animal referred to by Pliny:
"In Ethiopia,
```

```
    [...]

</TD>

<TD WIDTH=185>
which, actually, hang their heads like
ruminants to fight, but are not exposed to the
dangers of which Pliny wrote.
<BR><HR NOSHADE>
<FONT SIZE=6><B>The Dragon</B></FONT>
The imagination of the poets and artists of
antiquity gave birth to a
<BR><IMG SRC="dragon.gif" WIDTH=175><BR>
bizarre and frightening animal combining the
body and limbs of a lion, the wings of either
a bird or bat and the tail of a snake.

    [...]
</TD>
</TR>
</TABLE>
</DIV>
</BODY>
</HTML>
```

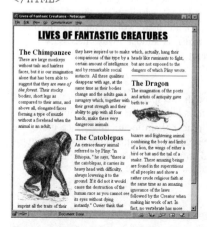

Figure 7.12: A table allows the layout of a printed newspaper to be imitated

There is no miracle: HTML does not allow true DTP, so we have to cheat a little! We want this page to be displayed in 640 × 480 format. To get a bit of a margin, we have made each column of equal width, i.e. 185 pixels. Thus, we have created a table without borders which has one row and three cells, each representing a single column of a page. The main title is an image created with a drawing program and a Trek-Monitor font with a size of 48.

We proceeded to input out text in the first cell handling breaks with `<BR>` or `<P>` and inserting images at the appropriate places. Between each of the three articles we put an `<HR>` tag without shade which acts as a separator. Titles were created with a larger font using the `<FONT SIZE=n>` container tags. Once this was completed we had one large column of text that we cut randomly in three so as to share the content among our three cells. By trial and error, moving a line here and there, we balanced it all up.

TABLES AND HTML EDITORS

As you can see, defining a precise layout with a table structure is not always easy. Graphical HTML editors make things easier to a certain extent. However, for intricate work, manipulating them becomes so complicated that it is almost always necessary to get your hands dirty and correct a few lines of the HTML code it has generated here and there.

On the other hand, although the specifications of the `<TABLE>` tag have now been fixed for a long time, it should be noted that the various browsers do not render them identically. Once more, we recommend checking what you have written with several systems (by way of hardware and software) before making it available to the public.

Chapter 8

Image maps, visitor counters, forms and frames

THE CONTENTS FOR THIS CHAPTER

- Creating image maps
- Using visitor counters
- Creating forms
- Displaying several windows at once with frames

We could leave it there with HTML given what we've learned so far: you now know enough to make sites that hold their own. However, image maps and counters are features which make a site more attractive and, as we said at the beginning of the book, nothing should be overlooked if you want to retain the occasional visitor.

CREATING IMAGE MAPS

The principle of (clickable) image maps is simple: you break down an image into zones which are easily identifiable and make each zone an internal or external link. In this way, instead of clicking on a text link, you click on an image. This is like having a menu of icons, but with far more subtlety.

The choice of image

Not all images are suitable for making image maps: they need to naturally break down into easily identifiable zones with clearly-defined shapes wherever possible: rectangles, circles or polygons.

A bad choice

For example, the picture of the chimpanzee that we used at the end of the previous chapter and which is reproduced in Figure 8.1 is not suitable at all: nothing is clearly separable.

Figure 8.1: This image is not suitable at all for making an image map

A reasonable choice

By contrast, Figure 8.2 is better suited to a site on the growing and eating of lettuce. It is simple to create and does not require any special drawing skills (although if you have some, you could certainly do something which looks better!). The font used is Stymie Light, which is different from most but easily readable (an essential criterion for a links menu). The overall title "To get great lettuce!" is in the Comic sans serif font. You will notice that the "Harvesting" link is placed in the middle and is displayed in a larger font size to attract attention. The various zones are individually coloured.

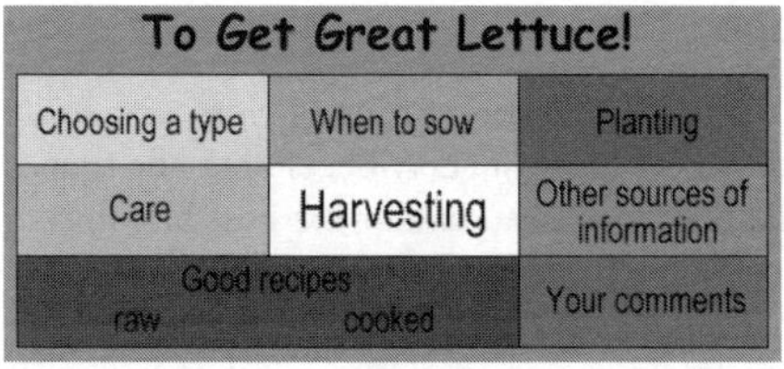

Figure 8.2: This image, although nothing special artistically, is better suited to creating a links menu

A better choice

Even so, it's hard to see how this presentation is better than the menu we saw at the end of the last chapter made up of small rectangular images in a table. It would be better to get rid of the frames and place the captions directly on a background which has the same colour. You would then have what is shown in Figure 8.3.

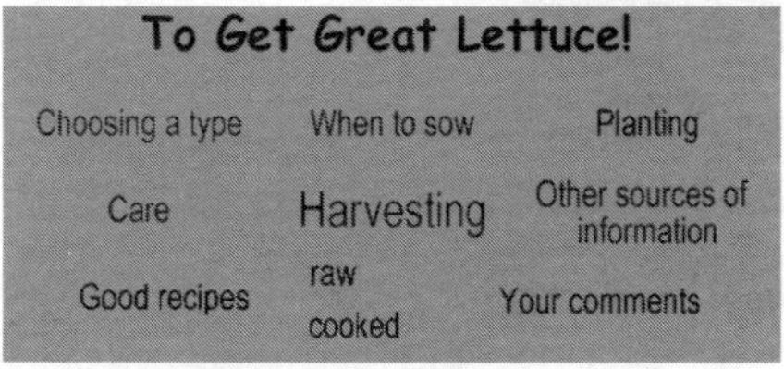

Figure 8.3: Improvements to our image map

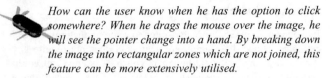

How can the user know when he has the option to click somewhere? When he drags the mouse over the image, he will see the pointer change into a hand. By breaking down the image into rectangular zones which are not joined, this feature can be more extensively utilised.

You could improve on the above by breaking down the sections somewhat randomly, slanting the text and making the corresponding zones circles, rectangles or polygons according to their shape and form.

An excellent image

If you have decided to provide the world of food lovers with some detailed information on where the best cuts of beef are to be found, Figure 8.4 is what you need. You can colour the best bits in red, those which are less good in pink and those which should be avoided in blue. Here, the image is perfect for the intended purpose and ideal for an image map. All the same, the division of the image will need to be done more carefully because, almost everywhere, you will need to use polygons, i.e. to define many points.

Figure 8.4: An excellent image map

Three possible implementations

Image maps are an old HTML creation and two of the most important partners ("adversaries" would probably be more apt) in this area, CERN (*European Centre for Nuclear Research* in France*)* and NCSA (*National Center for Supercomputing Applications*), each suggested their own standard; they were, of course, incompatible with each other. Curiously, these methods are as needlessly complicated as each other and call for a client server dialogue which we will broadly outline:

Not only are these methods incompatible, but you have to know, before you make your choice, which one is being used on your server. If you later move your site to another server, you may have to modify your HTML documents to adhere to the "standard" accepted by the new server.

1. The user clicks on an image map.

2. The point coordinates are sent to the server together with the name of the file attached to the image map by the browser.

3. The server launches a special program, generally *imagemap*.

4. This program searches through the file – which is a mapping table – for the URL of the link to be activated.

5. If the point is in one of the defined zones, the page at the corresponding URL is sent to the browser. If not, an error message is sent back.

6. If everything works out the correct page is displayed.

It took some time before someone at Netscape noticed that all this work could quite easily be carried out on the *client*, without having to call the *server*. Hence, the name *client side* was given to this new method.

In the beginning, the original methods continued to prevail because the browsers being used were not all able to interpret the new method. However, there need be no such complications now and so our study will leave them to one side and concentrate solely on the *client side* method. This does not require dialogue between the client and the server, which causes unnecessary loading on the Internet and lost time for the visitor.

Breaking down an image map

An image map contains zones known as *hot spots*. These may take three geometric shapes: a rectangle, a circle or a polygon. There is also a fourth zone, the *default* zone which has the curious property of not really existing. In fact, it allows a page to be loaded from a particular URL when the visitor clicks *outside* a real, defined zone. The contents of this page usually inform the visitor that he has pointed at the wrong place. To avoid erasing the page currently being displayed and subsequently needing to reload it, it is best to call upon a JavaScript script. We will come back to this in the next chapter.

Defining an image map

There are specialised programs for the creation of image maps. MapEdit and LiveImage, for PC amateurs, and the freeware WebMap (**mailto:rowland@city.net**), for those who swear by the Mac, are among the best known and most used. But there are alternatives. To understand the method of creation, we will explain how to write the necessary commands by hand with a normal text editor.

The first thing to do, of course, is to draw the image and then carefully denote the coordinates of the hot spots, expressed in pixels, which will be defined in a special container tag organised as a table and almost always placed in the HTML page where the image map is loaded:

- for a rectangle, the coordinates of the ends of the main diagonal;

- for a circle, the coordinates of the centre followed by the size of the radius;

- for a polygon, the coordinates of the points in order.

The container tag in which this table must be contained is <MAP NAME="name"> ... </MAP>. Within this are <AREA> markup commands, one for each hot spot to be defined. Each of these hot spots is defined as follow:

<area shape=type of hot spot coords="list of coordinates" href="anchor">

where *type of hot spot* may be rect, circle or polygon.

The image map will be loaded as a normal image by an <IMG> tag to which is added the attribute USEMAP followed by the name of the table describing the hot spots (from the container tag <MAP> ... </MAP>).

An example will show what is meant:

```
<HTML>
[...]
<BODY>
[...]
<IMG  SRC="lettuce.gif"  USEMAP="#lettuce"
BORDER="0">
[...]
<map  name="salades">
   <area  shape="rect"  coords="11,40,156,90"
     href="http://www.montruc.fr/semis.htm">
   <area  shape="polygon"
     coords="34,68,34,56,129,58,126,91,95,94,80,126,
     69,85"
     href="#rubrique_123">
   <area  shape="rect"coords="309,
   146,455,195"
     href="mailto:moimeme@montruc.fr">
   <area  shape="circle"  coords="221,66,24"
   href="#when_to_sow">
```

```
   <area shape="default" href="#erreur">
</map>
[...]
<A NAME="error">
Here an error in the choice of zone is
flagged
[...]
</BODY>
</HTML>
```

As you can see, you may have any type of link: internal or external. If you do not want to define the processing of an error for clicking outside the hot spots, instead of href= in the <AREA> markup command, you simply put the nohref; attribute. You could just as well point to a resource other than **http://**, as with **mailto:** in the previous example, (the protocol for sending e-mail).

You might have a situation where two hot spots partially overlap. In this case, it is the first which has been defined which will take precedence, because the browser explores the table of hot spots in the order that the <AREA> entries were created.

You can put comments inside a <MAP> ... </MAP> *container tag. They should be preceded by a hash character (#).*

The MapEdit utility

This is a shareware utility which is extremely easy to install. It handles the two older methods as well as the *client side* method. To create a table (or a definitions file), all you have to do is click on **File** and then **Open/Create**. In the dialog box which opens, choose the name of the HTML file (which must already exist) in which you wish to create the table and then click on **OK**.

A second dialog box gives the names of the images contained in the file and defined by the container tag <IMG>. You must then click on the one which will act as an image map and then on **OK**.

The formats recognised are GIF, JPEG and PNG.

The image is then loaded (Figure 8.5). The MapEdit toolbar offers, among others, three tools for defining the zone: a green square (the rectangle tool), a blue circle (the circle tool) and a red triangle (the polygon tool). Here is how to use them:

- To define a rectangle, you start by clicking on the green square in the toolbar. You then click on one apex of the rectangular hot spot and then again on the other end of the diagonal. Click again, and, in the dialog box which opens, type the URL or the anchor name corresponding to the zone you have just defined.

- To define a circle, you start by clicking on the blue circle in the toolbar. You then click at the centre of the hot spot and move the pointer until the circle that appears covers the zone you wish to define. You then click a second time and respond to the dialog box as before.

- To define a polygon, you start by clicking on the red triangle in the toolbar. You then click on each of the apexes of the polygon. For the last apex, you right click and proceed as before.

Figure 8.5: The Utility for making image maps, MapEdit

The on-line help is clear enough for us to be able to leave this subject and move on.

Using visitor counters

A visitor counter allows you to count the number of times a page in question has been downloaded. For this, it is necessary to have recourse to a server because the counter is created by a small file situated on the server. To use the contents of this file, a *general* server program must be executed (the Web author does not have to write a personal program) which will search the contents of this counter, increment it by one, turn it into an image made up of numbers and send this image to the person who requested it.

The counting function is therefore carried out by a link, although it is a direct link which takes the form of an image download. Here is an example, the result of which is shown in Figure 8.6:

```
<H3>
You are our
<IMG SRC="/cgi-bin/
counter?jdupont&font=stencil&width=4">
th visitor since 18 may 1996
</H3>
```

Figure 8.6: Displaying a visitor counter

In this command, here are what the various parameters correspond to:

- /cgi-bin/counter is the name of the server program which is called;

- ? is a separator;

- jdupont is the name of the personal directory where the counter is located;

- & is a separator;

- font=stencil specifies the style of the numeral images which will be used to make up the image of the counter returned. As you can see in Figure 8.6, the author has chosen a form of numerals which is similar to that of a pocket calculator;

- & is a separator; and

- width=4 specifies the number of numerals which the image of the counter will contain.

This is an example. In fact, the parameters used depend on how the access provider to which you subscribe implements it. You should therefore refer to your access provider on the specific details. Well-organised access providers offer an FAQ (frequently asked questions) containing all necessary information.

CREATING FORMS

Until now, there has not been dialogue between the client (the visitor) and the server (the access provider which hosts your site); it has been a monologue: the server talks and the client listens. However, you must have noticed while surfing the Web that sites which allow you to download a program often request that you first declare your identity. This proves that there is a way to send information from the client to the server. For this, you use a form.

A form works as follows:

- The Web page containing the form requests that the visitor provides certain information (name, *e-mail* address, etc.) in input boxes or completes check-boxes.

- At the end of these "HTML objects", a rectangular button is displayed which generally contains the word Submit or Send.

- When the client clicks on this button, the information provided in the input boxes is collated and sent to the server, accompanied by the name of a *special program written by the Web author* which resides in a special directory on the server. The name of this program is supplied by the author of the site in the initial tag of the form.

- When the server receives the message, it calls the named program and supplies it with the information it has received.

- The program processes this information and does with it what it thinks best: for example, it archives it. Generally, it sends a personalised acknowledgment of receipt to the client. For this, it creates an HTML file which is sent to the client's navigator and displayed.

To use a form, you must therefore:

- know how to program;

- be authorised to place a personal program on the hard disk of the Web server;

- be authorised to indirectly execute this program.

For obvious security reasons, the last two conditions more often than not give cause for concern on the part of access providers and so most of them do not authorise their subscribers to use forms. Usually, forms are used for commercial purposes and the access provider sub-processes the form, which solves any security problems. Personal Web pages may have to give this one a miss.

Finally, the first condition requires that the client knows a higher level programming language (generally PERL, sometimes C or C++), which is another reason for not putting a form in a personal page.

Fortunately, there is a simple way to get around these obstacles. Instead of being processed by a particular program on a server, the information received by the server is placed in an e-mail message and sent to the author at the address specified by him. For this, the <FORM> ... </FORM> container tag in which the form is placed should have the following form:

```
<FORM
ACTION="mailto:jdupont@myserver.co.uk">
[...]
</FORM>
```

where jdupont@myserver.co.uk is the e-mail address to which the information received by the form should be sent.

To extract this information you have to write a program. But nothing stops you from writing it in BASIC or any other simple language and, as this operation will be at the Web author's home, on his own hard disk, this does not risk creating a security breach on the service provider's server. The problem with this method is that it is impossible to send an appropriate real-time response to the information supplied by the visitor as is the case with the complete (and normal) type of form.

DISPLAYING SEVERAL WINDOWS AT ONCE WITH FRAMES

Using *frames*, you can display several windows on a screen, with some fixed and others reloadable. This function is particularly useful for keeping a navigation menu permanently displayed. The only problem with frames is that some users, attached to an old browser, will not be able to display them. However, as long as the author allows for it, there is a tag which allows the use of an entire group of ordinary Web pages. The price of this is that updates are tougher for the unfortunate author who must manage two different groups of pages.

It is not unreasonable now to reject browsers which do not support frames.

Structure of a Web site with frames

The first thing is to define the layout you want to give to your screen: how many zones will it be divided into?; what shape will these zones have?; and what will they contain? This geometric description will be translated by a special command, *frameset,* which should be contained in the first HTML file loaded when a visitor connects to your Web site. Figure 8.7 shows an example of the simple, traditional breakdown, in which the left zone is reserved for the navigation menu and the rest of the page for display. You will also encounter the layout shown in Figure 8.8, in which the small horizontal zone is used to display messages or advertisements for those who have sponsorship.

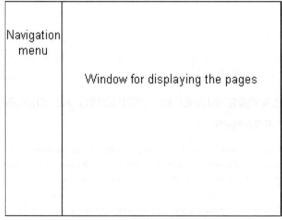

Figure 8.7: A very simple and traditional frame layout

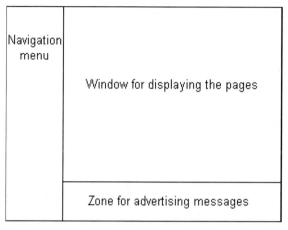

Figure 8.8: Another traditional frame layout

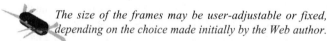
The size of the frames may be user-adjustable or fixed, depending on the choice made initially by the Web author.

Writing HTML tags for frames

There are two tags relating to frames: <FRAMESET> and <FRAME>. The first defines the actual breakdown of the space and the second the general properties of the zones thus defined. In addition, a third tag, <NOFRAMES>, is used as an aid for those browsers which need assistance with frames.

The *<FRAMESET>* container tag

For this first tag, here is the corresponding HTML document:

```
<HTML>
<HEAD>
<TITLE>A very simple frameset</TITLE>
</HEAD>
<FRAMESET COLS="25%,*">
```

```
        <FRAME SRC="menu.htm" NAME="menu">
        <FRAME SRC="main.htm" NAME="window">
</FRAMESET>
</HTML>
```

In all other files, it is pointless putting in the <TITLE> ... </TITLE> container tag because only that of the master file (the one which contains the breakdown of frames) will be displayed. Figure 8.9 shows how this is presented on the screen.

As you can see, this HTML file does not contain the <BODY> ... </BODY> container tag. It is replaced by <FRAMESET> ... </FRAMESET>, which plays the same role but only contains the definition of the break down. Here are the attributes you can meet in this container tag:

- ROWS=. Breakdown of the frameset in horizontal bands. This is a list of values in expressed pixels or as a percentage (in which case it is followed by the % character). With the exception of the first, the values may be expressed as an asterisk (*), which means "whatever is left over" or, if there is an *n*, "whatever is left over" divided by *n*).

Figure 8.9: A screen divided into two frames

- COLS=. Breakdown of the frameset in vertical bands. The values used are expressed as for ROWS.

By using ROWS and COLS in the same container tag, you get a breakdown in both directions which, in general, is not very aesthetic, as Figure 8.10 shows.

Figure 8.10: Such a breakdown is overly geometric and not very aesthetic

Nesting *<FRAMESET>* container tags

You can nest as many <FRAMESET> ... </FRAMESET> container tags as you wish. However, generally you do not nest more than 2 layers due to common sense and the size of the frames which you end up with. Here, for example, is the HTML document written to obtain the breakdown shown in Figure 8.11:

```
<HTML>
<HEAD>
<TITLE>A screen divided into three zones</TITLE>
</HEAD>
<FRAMESET COLS="25%,*">
    <FRAME SRC="menu.htm" NAME="menu">
    <FRAMESET ROWS="80%,*">
```

```
    <FRAME SRC="main.htm" NAME="window">
    <FRAME SRC="pub.htm" NAME="pub" NORESIZE
    SCROLLING=NO>
  </FRAMESET>
</FRAMESET>
</HTML>
```

Figure 8.11: A screen divided into three zones

The *<FRAME>* markup command

Here are the attributes which you may encounter in the <FRAME> container tag:

- SRC=. Specifies the name of the HTML document to load.

- NAME=. Gives a name to the relevant frame. This name is needed for specifying into which frame any new document designated by an anchor should be loaded.

- SCROLLING=. Does or does not allow the user to scroll through the contents of the window (possible values: NO, YES or AUTO).

- NORESIZE. Forbids the user from changing the size of the frame.

- `MARGINHEIGHT=` and `MARGINWIDTH=`. Allows a margin to be specified around the frame.

You may also see the variant spelling <FRAMES>. Browsers which recognise frames are generally not very strict on this question of spelling.

In the preceding example, you will note the use of the `NORESIZE` and `SCROLLING=NO` attributes which stop the visitor from removing the advertising banner.

The *<NOFRAMES>* container tag

Browsers which cannot interpret the `<FRAMESET>` ... `</FRAMESET>` container tag will often display a blank page. To avoid this, it is possible to specify "normal" HTML so that the user will at least be able to see something. Here is an example:

```
<HTML>
<HEAD>
<TITLE>A screen divided into three zones</TITLE>
</HEAD>
<FRAMESET COLS="25%,*">
      <FRAME SRC="menu.htm" NAME="menu">
      <FRAMESET ROWS="80%,*">
        <FRAME SRC="main.htm" NAME="window">
        <FRAME SRC="pub.htm" NAME="pub"
        NORESIZE SCROLLING=NO>
      </FRAMESET>
</FRAMESET>
<NOFRAMES>
<H2>Sorry, but to view this site you should
   use a browser which supports frames
</H2>
</NOFRAMES>
</HTML>
```

In reality, this does not go particularly far because, if you really want your whole site to be seen by browsers which do not support frames, you should write everything in duplicate, making allowance for completely different navigation systems for each of the two cases. This might initially be feasible, but updating such a system could quickly turn into a nightmare and, most of the time, one of these forms would be behind the other. Better to offer your polite apologies.

Loading a file inside a frame

In a Web site based on frames, you should indicate for each anchor the destination frame for each file to be loaded. It is the TARGET= attribute which should be used for this, as the following command shows:

```
<A HREF="montruc.htm" TARGET="window">My
tips</A>
```

When the visitor clicks on "My tips", the HTML document montruc.htm will be loaded into the window called window which is defined in our last example.

The TARGET attribute may take four especially reserved values which specify a particular destination into which the HTML document requested will be loaded:

- _blank: into a new window created for this circumstance;

- _self: into the window of the anchor;

- _parent: into the parent window of the current window or in the one from which the request is made if there is no upper level; or

- _top: into all space available in the browser window.

Chapter 9

Complete example of a Web site

THE CONTENTS FOR THIS CHAPTER

- Making general choices
- First draft
- Another version
- Another page

During this chapter we will put together a few ideas for planning and writing a complete site. As an example, we will construct a page devoted to an association for collectors of vintage French motorcycles: *The Gnome & Rhone Motorcycle Club (GRMC)*.

MAKING GENERAL CHOICES

One of the main problems for non-profit organisations is getting themselves known and, hence, recruiting members. Sharing a passion is not as easy as it might seem. As these organisations only have a meagre budget, there is no question of going to PR professionals. This being the case, an organisation should avoid being too ambitious in its design and layout plans, since all the work will probably be done by one person.

Hosting

It may seem odd to start with this worry, which normally comes last. However, for us it is of primary importance. Failure to find a free host might mean having to give up the idea. Good chairpersons of organisations generally consider that their members' subscription fees should primarily be used to provide services for them and not for extravagant PR, whether this is done via glossy newsletters or on a Web site.

Fortunately, it is now easy to find a host for your Web site, as you will learn in Chapter 11. Almost all Internet service providers include a certain amount of free Web space with a subscription. This allocation will usually be at least 5Mb (enough for most modestly-sized sites) and some ISPs are currently giving their members a massive 25Mb! Remember that your HTML pages themselves are usually tiny files, so hundreds of pages could be squeezed into 5Mb of Web space. The important thing is to be wary of using too many large images. As well as increasing the download times of your pages, these files will take up much larger chunks of your available space.

Subjects to be dealt with

For any organisation, you may wish to deal with a few of the following general matters, to which we will add a few more specific points of our own:

- the aims of the association;
- history;
- statutes;
- activities;
- membership;
- small ads;
- page of links to other organisations pursuing similar aims.

Restoration of vintage motorcycles requires the replacement of certain parts known as 'consumables': rubbers, decoration, gears, etc., which are obviously no longer marketed. The GRMC therefore offers its members not only restored parts but also technical documentation. In addition, it organises various public events: exhibitions, meetings, rallies, etc. Finally, it publishes five newsletters a year. All this leads us to add the following sections to our site:

- documentation;
- re-manufacture;
- calendar of events;
- newsletter.

Available documents

Our club has a large number of historic and technical documents to include on the site, as well as many photographs and drawings. Of course, none of this yet exists in electronic form. A scanner will therefore have to be used to digitise the images, and OCR (Optical Character Recognition) software will transcribe the textual documents. The price of A4-sized flatbed scanners has dropped considerably in recent years, and you can produce a good quality result from budget models at around £100 or less.

General structure of the site

Once these elements have been defined, you can see that we only need a simple branch structure, as each of the sections that we have defined is independent of the others. For the moment, it seems that a single HTML document for each section should be enough. From the home page, we imagine a links menu that leads to each of the pages. At the bottom of each page, a return to the home page would then allow the visitor to go to another section of his choice. This is the organisation shown in Figure 2.3 of Chapter 2.

FIRST DRAFT

Before going any further, we must equip ourselves with an HTML editor (go back to Chapter 4 if needed) and put together a few commands just to get an idea of the result. There is no point going further than the home page at the moment. Later, we will create the links needed to visit the sections on offer.

The home page

In a few minutes we have a file that we will call GRMC1.HTM which, when loaded by a browser, gives us what is shown in Figure 9.1.

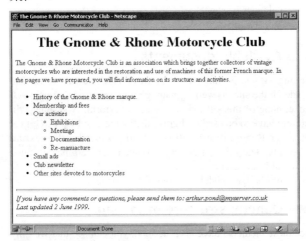

Figure 9.1: The first tryout

Objectively speaking, quite a few criticisms can be made:

- It's not very engaging: presentation of the club is dull, the style is flat and overall it is too brief.

- The page lacks personality.

- The sections are presented without any order.

- There is a typing error (*re-manuacture*).

The first few improvements

We will bring a bit of order to our sections and, at the same time, improve out text presentation with a few images. Any group of people, whether business-oriented or otherwise, has a logo which embodies its personality. GRMC is no exception and uses a reproduction of an advertising document from the 30s (see Figure 9.2). Using a scanner, we will digitise it in a reduced format (190 × 280, i.e. 27 KB) so that the download time is not too long. Then, with a graphics program such as PaintBrush or Paint Shop Pro, we will extract a silhouette (see Figure 9.3) which will be coloured in light grey so that the text is not hidden and which will be used to create a mosaic style background. The background of this GIF image will be defined as transparent.

Figure 9.2: The GRMC logo

***Figure 9.3: The silhouette which will be used to create a
background to the page***

In addition, we will use an icon of about 30 x 30 pixels to symbolise
e-mail, and make a few stylistic corrections. Without too much
attention to the layout, what we get is shown in Figure 9.4.

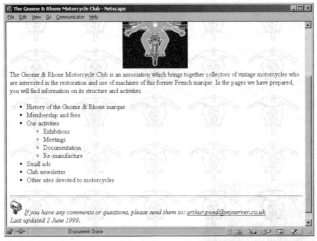

Figure 9.4: The first improvements to the GRMC home page

Other improvements

Firstly, our logo is much too large compared to the text, since the
home page is clearly larger than the size of the screen (the format
displayed is 632 × 585 pixels). Making the reader scroll around the
home page to see the important parts should be avoided at all costs.
We will therefore try to place the logo and text side by side. The
result is shown in Figure 9.5.

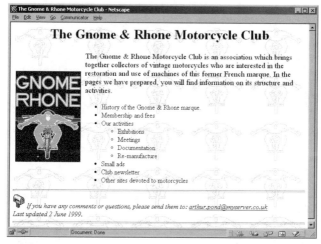

Figure 9.5: The home page looks better like this

This time, it is altogether more harmonious and, above all, smaller. We have used a font size of 4 (in HTML units) to display the short text so that it comes up better. The use of the `<TABLE>` container tag has allowed us to place the logo and all the text side by side as you can see in the extract of code below:

```
<HTML>
<HEAD>
  <TITLE>The Gnome &amp; Rhone Motorcycle
Club</TITLE>
</HEAD>

<BODY BACKGROUND="grmc.jpg">

<DIV ALIGN=CENTER>
<H1>The Gnome &amp; Rhone Motorcycle Club</H1>
</DIV>

<TABLE ALIGN="CENTER">
<TR>
<TD>
```

```
<IMG SRC="logo.gif" WIDTH="158" HEIGHT="212"
ALT="The GRMC logo">
</TD>

<TD>
<FONT SIZE="4">
The Gnome &amp; Rhone Motorcycle Club is an
association which brings together collectors
of vintage motorcycles who are interested in
the restoration and use of machines of this
former French marque.  In the pages we have
prepared, you will find information on its
structure and activities.
</FONT>
<UL>
<LI>History of the Gnome &amp; Rhone marque.
<LI>Membership and fees
<LI>Our activities
     <UL>
     <LI>Exhibitions
     <LI>Meetings
     <LI>Documentation
     <LI>Re-manufacture
     </UL>
<LI>Small ads
<LI>Club newsletter
<LI>Other sites devoted to motorcycles
</UL>
</TD>
</TR>
</TABLE>

<HR SIZE="3" ALIGN="CENTER">

<ADDRESS>
<IMG SRC="email.gif" WIDTH="30" HEIGHT="33"
ALT="Email">
 If you have any comments or questions,
please send them to: <A HREF="mailto:arthur.
pond@myserver.co.uk">arthur.pond@myserver.co.
uk</A>
<BR>
```

```
Last updated 2 June 1999.
</ADDRESS>

<HR SIZE="3" ALIGN="CENTER">

</BODY>
</HTML>
```

Indicating the size of images to be downloaded allows the page to be displayed faster as the browser knows in advance how in much space to prepare in the window and is able to display the text while continuing to download images. Most good HTML editors automatically insert these indications.

You will notice that we have always used the ALT= option in the image markup commands so that visitors who have deactivated image download still have some idea of what they're missing.

Should we go further?

Although the site has the advantage of being clear, it must be said that graphically it clearly lacks something. We could certainly improve it by asking some members of the Club who are known for their artistic talent to give us a more aesthetic model. But is this really necessary? We're not competing for a Web Oscar and the people we are looking to attract are more concerned about the contents of our pages than their presentation, as long as it is clear.

Don't forget that the contents are more important than the container. In a site which is purely functional (i.e. the site of a club which does not have artistic aims), there is a balance to be found between the attractiveness of the page and the value of the information it offers.

That is why we have chosen to stay with what we've got for the home page. The only improvement that we will carry out is the use of a lightly coloured background using the BGCOLOR= attribute. As this book is printed in black and white, it is pointless displaying the result thus obtained.

ANOTHER VERSION

We saw in Chapter 8 that it is not easy to decide whether or not to use frames. If you think that the visitors that you will attract use recent browsers, you might risk it. Figure 9.6 shows another version of the same home page in which the left frame contains a menu made from graphical elements. Why this added complication if the menu is to be displayed as text? For two reasons: firstly, because what is displayed in this way does not depend on the fonts actually installed on the visitor's machine and, secondly, because the use of a narrow font allows us more space for the right window which contains the useful information.

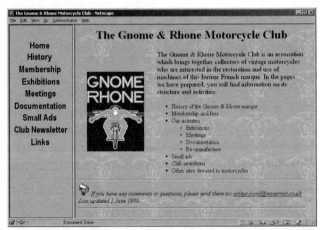

Figure 9.6: Version of the home page using frames

Here is the coding for the three files necessary to construct this home page:

- The frameset definition file, INDEX.HTM, which contains a short explanatory text for the use of visitors with a browser that does not support frames.

- The navigation file, NAVIGA.HTM, which contains anchors required to access the various sections offered.

- The general display file, PRESENTA.HTM, which contains the short piece of text to be displayed on the home page proper.

INDEX.HTM
```
<HTML>
<HEAD>
  <TITLE>The Gnome &amp; Rhone Motorcycle
Club</TITLE>
</HEAD>

<FRAMESET COLS="200, *">
     <FRAME NAME="naviga" SRC="naviga.htm">
     <FRAME NAME="presenta"
SRC="presenta.htm">
</FRAMESET>

<NOFRAMES>
<BODY BACKGROUND="grmc.gif">
<HR>
<B>Sorry, but this site can only be viewed
with a browser that is able to recognise
<I>frames</I>. We recommend that you use
version 3.0 or higher of Microsoft Internet
Explorer or Netscape Navigator.</B>
<HR>
</NOFRAMES>

</HTML>
```

The <NOFRAMES> container tag contains the text which will be displayed to warn users with a browser which does not support frames. Figure 9.7 shows what is obtained by using the latest version of Mosaic for Windows (dating from the end of March 1996).

NAVIGA.HTM
```
<HTML>
<HEAD>
  <TITLE>The Gnome &amp; Rhone Motorcycle
Club</TITLE>
</HEAD>
<BODY BGCOLOR="#55EECC">
```

```
<BASE  TARGET="presenta">
<IMG  SRC="empty.gif"  ALT="">
 <A HREF="presenta.htm"><IMG SRC="home.gif"
ALT="Home"  BORDER="0"></A>
 <A HREF="history.htm"><IMG SRC="history.gif"
ALT="History"  BORDER="0"></A>
 <A HREF="join.htm"><IMG SRC="join.gif"
ALT="Membership"  BORDER="0"></A>
 <A HREF="exhibit.htm"><IMG SRC="exhibit.gif"
ALT="Exhibitions"  BORDER="0"></A>
 <A HREF="meetings.htm"><IMG
SRC="meetings.gif"  ALT="Meetings"
BORDER="0"></A>
 <A HREF="docs.htm"><IMG SRC="docs.gif"
ALT="Documentation"  BORDER="0"></A>
 <A HREF="ads.htm"><IMG SRC="ads.gif"
ALT="Small  Ads"  BORDER="0"></A>
 <A HREF="news.htm"><IMG SRC="news.gif"
ALT="Club  Newsletter"  BORDER="0"></A>
 <A HREF="links.htm"><IMG SRC="links.gif"
ALT="Links"  BORDER="0"></A>
</BODY>
</HTML>
```

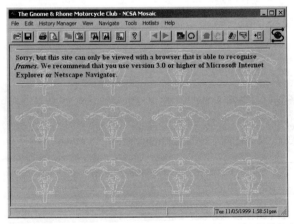

Figure 9.7: Those with a browser which does not recognise frames will only see this message

Chapter 9 : Complete example of a Web site

Here, the ALT attribute is necessary because, without it, visitors
who have deactivated image download will have no way whatsoever
of moving around. Furthermore, what is displayed (see Figure 9.8)
will not be very presentable because of the space occupied by the
text that replaces it. The file EMPTY.GIF is used to shift the display
downwards to centre all the menu entries more effectively.

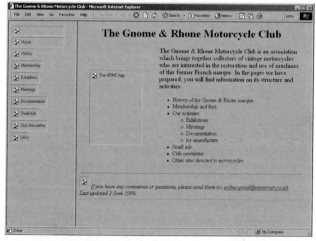

*Figure 9.8: What the visitor will see who has deactivated
image downloads*

PRESENTA.HTM
```
<HTML>
<HEAD>
  <TITLE>The Gnome &amp; Rhone Motorcycle
Club</TITLE>
</HEAD>

<BODY BACKGROUND="grmc.gif"
BGCOLOR="#55EECC">

<DIV ALIGN=CENTER>
<H1>The Gnome &amp; Rhone Motorcycle Club</H1>
```

```
</DIV>
<TABLE ALIGN="CENTER" BORDER="1">
<TR>

<TD VALIGN=TOP WIDTH=20> </TD>

<TD>
     <IMG SRC="logo.gif" WIDTH="158"
HEIGHT="212" ALT="The GRMC logo">
</TD>

<TD WIDTH=40> </TD>

<TD>
<FONT SIZE="4">

The Gnome &amp; Rhone Motorcycle Club is an
association which brings together collectors
of vintage motorcycles who are interested in
the restoration and use of machines of this
former French marque. In the pages we have
prepared, you will find information on its
structure and activities.

</FONT>
<UL>
<LI>History of the Gnome &amp; Rhone marque.
<LI>Membership and fees
<LI>Our activities
     <UL>
     <LI>Exhibitions
     <LI>Meetings
     <LI>Documentation
     <LI>Re-manufacture
     </UL>
<LI>Small ads
<LI>Club newsletter
<LI>Other sites devoted to motorcycles
</UL>
</TD>
</TR>
```

```
</TABLE>

<HR SIZE="3" ALIGN="CENTER">
<ADDRESS>
<IMG SRC="email.gif" WIDTH="30" HEIGHT="33"
ALT="Email"> If you have any comments or
questions, please send them to: <A HREF=
"mail to:arthur.pond@myserver.co.uk">arthur.
pond@myserver.co.uk</A><BR>
Last updated 2 June 1999.
</ADDRESS>
<HR SIZE="3" ALIGN="CENTER">
</BODY>
</HTML>
```

Figure 9.9, obtained by giving the BORDER attribute of the
<TABLE> tag the value 1, shows how to use two additional empty
cells to better separate the text and the logo.

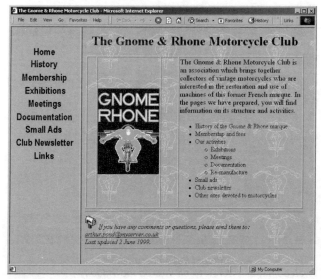

Figure 9.9: Empty cells in a table may improve the layout

To properly benefit from a site using frames, the visitor should be able to display a screen of at least 800 × 600 pixels. A smaller screen would entail excessive use of the scrolling bars.

ANOTHER PAGE

The page entitled "Motorcycle Gallery" displays the menu reproduced in Figure 9.10, in which the visitor may choose to display an image from the twelve on offer. This is a special case, because we are actually dealing with a sub-menu which must be managed locally without using a frame structure. Each of the twelve gallery pages must therefore contain a small linking image which returns the visitor to the "Gallery" sub-menu. The visitor who wants to exit this sub-menu has the choice of clicking directly on the menu in the left frame. Figure 9.11 shows an example of the contents of one of the entries in the sub-menu.

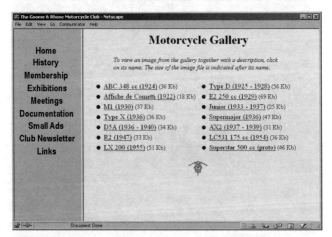

Figure 9.10: A traditional links menu allows each of the twelve images offered to be viewed individually

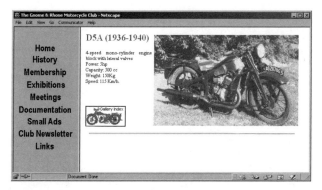

Figure 9.11: Each of the twelve sub-menu pages has a "back" arrow for returning to the menu list

Here again, we see that using the <TABLE> container tag without a border makes for effective layout.

Chapter 10

Scripts, style sheets and dynamic HTML

THE CONTENTS FOR THIS CHAPTER

- Java
- ActiveX
- Style sheets
- Dynamic HTML

With the exception of forms, the HTML documents studied so far have included only passive elements that can only be displayed or reproduced (in the case of multimedia files). This limits their power somewhat, but it does make them highly secure. Firstly, you know exactly what is being stored on your PC, and, secondly, the user cannot do anything dangerous. Even a virus cannot penetrate by this method, except of course when a file is transferred. Unfortunately, this is a routine risk to which you are exposed if you look for files in more out-of-the-way places.

In order to give more versatility to HTML documents that you have loaded, Sun Microsystems, the well-known manufacturer of workstations, created a language called Java. For its part, Netscape offered JavaScript, which was not so ambitious. Finally, Microsoft, not to be left out, created ActiveX.

Elsewhere, W3C, the official authority in charge of implementing the HTML language, published preliminary specifications for HTML 4.0 which included many new features and, in particular, *style sheets*. A working group was set up to define *Dynamic HTML*, in relation to which Netscape and Microsoft had already started to carry out different implementations in their respective browsers.

Each of these five themes would require a book twice as thick (or more) as this one for an in-depth analysis. You will not, therefore, be surprised to learn that we will only be outlining these matters. However, if you are interested then the bibliography in Chapter 12 lists a few useful publications and sites.

JAVA

The Java logo is a cup of steaming coffee because, for Americans, Java is a common word denoting coffee.

■■■■ A short history

Java was born at the start of the 1990s out of Sun Microsystems' idea to create a language to control consumer electronics devices. Then came the Web and its proliferation, of which we are all aware. In response, Sun had the idea of modifying this language, which had come to a sudden demise, so that it would animate (in the broader sense) static HTML documents sent between servers and clients. The first implementation was in HotJava, a browser for Sun computers. As is well known, in computing, even more so than in other areas, "new is beautiful". It had been quite a long time (five years or more?) since the birth of a new language. It was therefore greeted with great enthusiasm.

Helped by faultless marketing, the popularity of this language became universal and when more level-headed minds noted its many security flaws (which would allow, among other things, manipulation of the contents of the user's hard drive) and how slowly it ran, they had difficulty making themselves heard. Although, since then, security has been increased, the speed (or, rather, slowness) has not substantially improved.

The characteristics of the language

The structure of the Java language is similar to that of C++. It is effectively C++ with the pointers and basic memory management removed, which somewhat simplifies the writing but does not make it accessible to the Sunday programmer used to cobbling together ten lines of BASIC to run short programs.

The interest created by Java rests on its complete portability. Java is a semi-interpreted language. Starting with the source file, compilation generates an intermediate code1 (as with Pascal's P-code). It is this code that is exported and, for example, sent to a Web client. In this form, the code cannot be executed because it does not correspond to the machine code of any computer. It must therefore be interpreted, which is the browser's job. The browser must therefore include, in addition to its usual functions, a *Java virtual machine,* which is nothing other than an interpreter which analyses each of the *meta instructions* of the intermediate code and executes the functions that it describes. A little like a crude BASIC interpreter would.

Programs written in Java are called applets (nothing to do with the Macintosh!)

Incorporating applets into a Web page

To do this, the first implementations used a special container tag, `<APPLET> ... </APPLET>`, which contained attributes describing the applet to be loaded. Here is an example:

```
<HTML>
<HEAD>
<TITLE>Example of how to incorporate a Java
applet</TITLE>
</HEAD>
<BODY>
<APPLET CODE=Salut HEIGHT=50 WIDTH=150>
</APPLET>
</BODY>
</HTML>
```

HTML 4.0 has demoted this container tag to the rank of HTML objects whose use is 'not advised' and offers in its place the `<OBJECT> ... </OBJECT>` container tag which is, unfortunately, not sufficiently used in navigators.

Attributes give the name of the applet and the size of the window that it will use to display in the browser's window. There are a handful of these. Inside the `<APPLET>` container tag, there is a series of `<PARAM>` markup commands which, using `NAME/VALUE` attribute pairs, allows arguments to be assigned to the applet.

An example of an applet

We will take the simplest example there is, inspired by the traditional *Hello, world!* program which is well known to those who adore K&R (Kernighan & Ritchie, the immortal creators of C!).

```
import java.applet.*;
import java.awt.*;
public class Salut extends Applet
{ public void paint(Graphics g)
  { g.drawstring("Hello, World !", 20, 10);
  }
}
```

Programming in Java is beyond the ability of the beginner. Even adding ready-made applets to a Web page is not simple. Java is often used to create stylish site-navigation alternatives to hyperlinks and linked images, the there's an example at **http:// www.ohmsystems.com/welcome.html**.

In summary

To understand and interpret an applet, the browser must have a Java virtual machine at its disposal. This is the case, in particular, with Netscape Navigator and Internet Explorer, as well as Sun's HotJava. However, we have already mentioned several times that many Web surfers are attached to older browsers with which they feel comfortable, but which will not necessarily understand Java. This being the case, if you use Java, you will limit the number of visitors who will be able to wonder at what your applets do. In addition, browsers have a configuration option which allows (for security reasons, for example) the Java virtual machine to be turned off. Cautious people make frequent use of this option.

JavaScript

JavaScript is a small scripting language more or less based on Java and invented by Netscape.

A script is a small program generally written in a specific language and commonly used to carry out certain system functions.

The characteristics of the language

JavaScript is an entirely interpreted language, which makes it compatible with all machines, as long as the browser has a JavaScript interpreter. This is not really an object-oriented language, but more a language which is *object-tinted* and whose aims are limited. The following table summarises a few of the characteristics comparing Java and JavaScript:

Java	JavaScript
Created by Sun Microsystems	Created by Netscape
Compiled on the server	Interpreted by the client
Strongly object-oriented	Object-tinted
Generalised notion of inheritance	No inheritance
Code independent of the HTML document	Code included in the HTML document
Strongly typed language	Poorly typed language
Allows real applications to be written	Limited to small procedures
Average security	High security
Complicated (C++ level)	A well-behaved child (hardly evolved beyond BASIC)
Not very fast execution	Fairly slow execution
Aimed mainly at professionals	Accessible to amateurs

As far as JavaScript's syntax is concerned, although it borrows a few elements from the C language, it remains simple. There are no pointers, semi-colons, input/output or memory management, but there are loop structures and only two types of variable, number and character strings, which may be easily converted from one to the other. A JavaScript script can easily access the elements of the HTML document which contains it because the language was specifically designed to cohabit with HTML.

▰▰▰ Incorporating scripts into a Web page

The `<SCRIPT> ... </SCRIPT>` container tag is used for this purpose. It contains all the uncoded script instructions. These may be executed when the HTML document is loaded, but the functions contained in a script may also be called from an HTML document. One of the usual functions of scripts consists, for example, of verifying what the user types into a form and checking if it is valid. If everything is correct, the form is sent to the server. Otherwise, a message is displayed to advise the user and indicate what should be corrected. This method is easier (it does not load the Internet so much) than the old procedure which involved calling a CGI script situated on the server.

For this, a script is able to create small supplementary windows to display its messages so as not to eat into the layout of the HTML document in which it is located. Here is an example of a very simple script, whose functioning is identical to the applet that we presented for Java:

```
<HEAD>
<SCRIPT  LANGUAGE="JavaScript">
<!--
function salut()
{ alert("Hello World!")
}
// -->
</SCRIPT>
</HEAD>
```

The script is called by clicking on a form button:

```
<BODY>
<FORM NAME="form1">
<INPUT TYPE="button" NAME="bout1"
VALUE="Salut!" onClick="salut()">
</FORM>
</BODY>
```

The result is shown in Figure 10.1. A comparison of the two versions (the one written in Java and this one) speaks for itself!

Figure 10.1: A JavaScript version of "Hello world"

An example of JavaScript

Because of its close links with HTML, we think JavaScript is the best way to add things to a Web page. As an example, we will use a semi-perpetual calendar (only valid for this decade). When the user loads this calendar's Web page, what is shown in Figure 10.2 will be displayed. After having chosen the year and the month, the user clicks on the Display button and a small window opens (Figure 10.3) in which a perfectly laid out calendar for the current month is displayed. By clicking on the Erase button, the small window disappears. The following coding shows the script. Unfortunately, there is not space here to comment on it in more detail.

```
<HTML>
<HEAD>
<TITLE>A (Semi-) Perpetual Calendar</TITLE>

<SCRIPT LANGUAGE="JavaScript">
<!--
ever=true
shift=0
function create(year, month)
{ if (year== -1)
  { cal.close()
    return
  }
```

```
   days = new Array ("Monday", "Tuesday",
"Wednesday", "Thursday", "Friday", "Saturday",
"Sunday")
   month = new Array (31, 28, 31, 30, 31, 30,
31, 30, 31, 30, 31)
   month_name = new Array ("January",
"February", "March", "April", "May",
"June", "July", "August", "September",
"October", "November", "December")
   years = new Array (0, 1, 2, 4, 5, 6, 0, 2,
3, 4, 5)
   // 90 91 92 93 94 95 96 97 98 99 00

   actual_year = 1990 + year
   if ((actual_year % 4 == 0) && (actual_
year %100 != 0)
        ||(actual_year % 400 == 0)) leap_year = 1
else leap_year = 0
   correction = month > 1? leap_year: 0
   day_number = years[year] +  correction
   for (i=0; i<month; i++)
    day_number += month[i]

   weekday = day_number % 7
// ----------------------------------------
   if (ever) ever =false
   cal = open("", "ABCD","height=220,width=
450,scrollbars=yes")
   cal.document.write("<TABLE BORDER=1>")
   cal.document.write("<CAPTION><B>" +
month_name[month] +  " - " +
                      (year+1990) +  "</B></
CAPTION>")
   cal.document.write("<TR>")
   for (i=0; i<7; i++)
    cal.document.write("<TH WIDTH=67>" +
days[i] +  "</TH>")
   cal.document.write("</TR>")
   for (i=0, debut=1, bascule=false; i<6;
i++)
   { cal.document.write("<TR ALIGN=center>")
    for (j=0; j<7; j++)
```

```
    { if (i == 0 && j == weekday) rocker =
true
      if (rocker) cal.document.write("<TD
WIDTH=70>" + debut++ + "</TD>")
              else cal.document.write("<TD
WIDTH=70> </TD>")
      if ((Month!= 1 && debut >month[Month]) ||
         (Month== 1 && debut > month[Month]
+  leap_year)) rocker = false
    }
    cal.document.write("</TR>")
    if (! rocker) break
  }
  cal.document.write("</TABLE><HR>")
  cal.scroll(0, shift)
  shift += 300
}
// -->
</SCRIPT>
</HEAD>

<BODY onUnload="window.create(-1)">
<DIV ALIGN=CENTER><H1>My Calendar of the
Decade</H1>

<FORM NAME="CAL">
Choose a year:
<SELECT NAME="year" SIZE=5>
<OPTION VALUE=0> 1990
<OPTION VALUE=1> 1991
<OPTION VALUE=2> 1992
<OPTION VALUE=3> 1993
<OPTION VALUE=4> 1994
<OPTION VALUE=5> 1995
<OPTION VALUE=6> 1996
<OPTION VALUE=7> 1997
<OPTION VALUE=8 SELECTED> 1998
<OPTION VALUE=9> 1999
<OPTION VALUE=10> 2000
```

```
</SELECT>
and a month:
<SELECT NAME="month" SIZE=5>
<OPTION VALUE=1> January
<OPTION VALUE=2> February
<OPTION VALUE=3> March
<OPTION VALUE=4> April
<OPTION VALUE=5> May
<OPTION VALUE=6 SELECTED> June
<OPTION VALUE=7> July
<OPTION VALUE=8> August
<OPTION VALUE=9> September
<OPTION VALUE=10> October
<OPTION VALUE=11> November
<OPTION VALUE=12> December
</SELECT>
<P>
<INPUT TYPE="button" NAME="choice"
VALUE="Display"

onClick="create(document.CAL.year.selected

Index,document.CAL.month.selectedIndex)">
<INPUT TYPE="Clear" VALUE="Erase" NAME="nul"
   onClick="create(-1)">
</FORM>
</DIV>
</BODY>
</HTML>
```

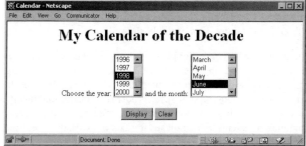

Figure 10.2: The calendar's home page

Monday	Tuesday	Wednesday	Thursday	Friday	Saturday	Sunday
1	2	3	4	5	6	7
8	9	10	11	12	13	14
15	16	17	18	19	20	21
22	23	24	25	26	27	28
29	30					

Figure 10.3: What a user sees when they choose the year and month

Although this script executes perfectly with Netscape Navigator 4.04, it's not the same with Internet Explorer 4.0 which reports errors because it does not recognise one of the (perfectly valid) commands. Thus, this shows the danger of incorporating scripts in an HTML document without first testing them with the two most widely used browsers on the market.

In summary

JavaScript is really a language designed for the Web since it cannot exist outside an HTML document. Using it is easy and, although it has nowhere near the "power" of Java, its various functions work well in an HTML context. As for Java, it cannot be understood by all browsers, some of them not using the appropriate interpreter. Our two main players, Netscape Navigator and Internet Explorer, understand it perfectly, but interpret some of the instructions differently as the previous example showed.

In terms of security, JavaScript is much less dangerous than Java, the worst it can do being to crash the machine on which it is running without causing damage to the files in it. Not being designed to carry out calculations, its slow speed is not really a fault. And finally, the ease with which it can be written does not require great programming talents, which makes it much more easily accessible to the Web author than Java.

ACTIVEX

This is a language created by Microsoft who (apparently) did not want to be outdone by Sun. Its main drawback is that it is really only supported by Internet Explorer. There is a plug-in for Netscape but, in the opinion of experts, it does not run as it should. What is more, even with Microsoft, ActiveX is only fully usable under Windows 95/98 and Windows NT. There are also implementations for the Macintosh and a few UNIX rehashes.

ActiveX is based on the use of 'prefabricated' modules (ActiveX controls) together with a scripting language. In one of its Web pages about ActiveX, Microsoft gives the following example using the ActiveX control IEPopup together with VBScript which is a language based on Visual Basic (also from Microsoft):

```
    [...]
<INPUT TYPE="button" NAME="Run"
VALUE="Run Popup Menu"
  ALIGN=LEFT>
<SCRIPT LANGUAGE="VBScript">
Sub Run_onClick
call IEPopup.PopUp()
End Sub
Sub IEPopup_Click(ByVal x)
Alert "You have clicked on element no.:" &x
Call IEPopup.RemoveItem(x)
call IEPopup.AddItem("Element replaced!", x)
End Sub
</SCRIPT>
    [...]
```

Here, the problem of portability does not arise as only Internet Explorer is capable of interpreting Visual Basic and ActiveX.

STYLE SHEETS

In a word processor, a style sheet allows you to define a certain type of layout for a given category of document (letter, curriculum vitae, invoice, technical note, etc.). The style sheet is saved at the same time as the document, so that if you send the file of a document to someone they may print it in the same way you do.

HTML was designed to describe the structure of documents and not their layout. However, the popularity of the Web meant that HTML escaped from its creators and was used for purposes for which it was not intended. To create sites that were pleasing to the eye, Web authors turned certain tags away from their original use (<TABLE>, for example) and browser developers created extensions to the language. This has lead to a certain confusion, a page that was perfect in Netscape Navigator becoming unsightly with Internet Explorer.

Style sheets were the solution suggested by W3C to allow Web authors to express themselves. Without achieving the power of PostScript or Acrobat, they allow precise page layouts which are almost perfectly reproducible.

Principles of cascading style sheets

Of all the possible models for style sheets, W3C decided on CSS (*Cascading Style Sheet*). "Cascading" conveys the idea that information coming from many style sheets may be reconstituted to define the layout which will be applied to an HTML document. Precise rules define what prevails in the case of contradictory specifications when several style sheets are brought together.

There are three possible sources of style sheets. They may be incorporated into an HTML document with the <STYLE> ... </STYLE> container tag inside the head section (<HEAD>). They may be contained in a separate document with the extension .CSS which will be loaded by an HTML command in the document to be laid out. Finally, they can ("will be able to" would be more accurate) be incorporated into one browser or another. If that is not enough, it is always possible to modify a style bit by bit.

What does a style sheet contain?

A style sheet consists of a series of *rules* which may be applied to the various levels of an HTML document, whether to all the tags of a given type (it is possible, for example, to specify that everything contained in an <H3> tag should be displayed in red), or to a *class* of elements defined using the CLASS= attribute, or solely to a certain tag marked with an identifier (the ID attribute). To clarify this, here is an example of a style sheet contained inside an HTML document:

```
<HTML>
<HEAD>
<TITLE>A simple style sheet</TITLE>

<STYLE>
<!--
H2 {font-family: Arial Black;
    color: #FF0000; text-align: center}
I  {color: green; font-family: "courier
new"}
-->
</STYLE>
</HEAD>

<BODY>
<H2>This is the title of the page</H2>
Every word in <I>italics</I> will be
displayed in green, except if you use the
&lt;SPAN&gt; tag as in:
<BR>
The
<I><SPAN STYLE="color:blue">
Mediterranean</SPAN></I> sea is blue.
<HR>
</BODY>
</HTML>
```

Here, the style sheet has two rules. This first indicates that <H2> titles should be centred and displayed in red with the Ariane Black font. The second requires that all words in italics (placed inside the `<I> ... </I>` container tag) should be displayed with the `Courier New` font and in green. However, in the last sentence, it was decided that the word "Mediterranean" should be displayed in blue and not green. The result is shown (without colour) in Figure 10.4.

Figure 10.4: A simple style sheet

Properties of style sheets

The *properties* of a style sheet are comparable to the attributes of HTML tags. They are attached to various elements in the HTML document: structure, layout, presentation, etc. It is not easy to establish a precise classification because certain properties are involved with several categories. However, it is possible to give a rough breakdown into the following classes, which we will briefly review.

Blocks

Any HTML element may be thought of as being placed in a rectangular block which may be surrounded by a border. The latter comprises two zones: the *margin* (the outermost) and the *padding* (closer to the block itself). These zones may have backgrounds of a different colour or may be transparent. This makes it possible to easily create margins in the four directions. The borders themselves may take on different forms and, in particular, give an appearance of being etched or in relief.

The concept of the block is an extension of ALIGN="left" and ALIGN="right" which, when used with the <IMG> tag, make it possible to inlay an image in text. Here, you may inlay text within text or overlay blocks of text.

Images

Although the <IMG> tag was retained in HTML 4.0, a new tag, <OBJECT>, makes the idea more prominent. An image is still thought of as a rectangular block: in this regard, style sheets don't offer anything new. Images may be made transparent (which is not to be confused with the notion of a transparent GIF image) and may be superimposed on text. A mosaic background no longer necessarily applies to the whole page: for example, a different background may be specified. The mosaic effect itself may be repeated horizontally, vertically or (as is usual) in both directions. The background may be fixed or moved at the same time as the text.

Finally, the position of an image in a page may be controlled absolutely or relatively by a system of rectangular coordinates, which allows precise layout.

Colours

This is mainly for backgrounds which use softened colours. Colours are still expressed in the same way: either by conventional names or by RGB (red, green, blue) elements.

Text and fonts

It is text which gains most from style sheets. This is only to be expected given that, in a Web page, it is the *content* that is most important. It is possible, of course, to specify a font and, better still, you can control the space between characters and their horizontal alignment with respect to the normal base line. Between a "normal" font and a "bold" font, there are now several degrees of character thickness.

Flashing makes its official debut (it is no longer only a Netscape extension). It is possible to control positive or negative indentation in a paragraph or in the first line only. Finally, you can create ornamental characters (the first letter of the first word of the paragraph larger than the rest of the paragraph).

Lists

These have not benefited from many improvements. The most notable is the possibility of using images other than the traditional bullet point (a circle, disk or square) in bulleted lists.

Others

The greatest innovation is, without doubt, the flexibility in positioning elements in the page and arranging how they are to be superimposed (which allows mask or transparency effects to be handled). Also of note is the possibility of displaying consecutive spaces by taking account of how many there are.

Example of use

We have chosen to present the famous poem by Herman Melville, "Monody", in a page layout which is fairly simple, but difficult to obtain without the use of style sheets. Figure 10.5 shows the result obtained in Netscape Navigator which responds to the style sheet commands. By contrast, Internet Explorer takes too many liberties and too many properties are not recognised (or are badly interpreted).

```
<HTML>
<HEAD>
```

```
<TITLE>Monody</TITLE>
</HEAD>

<STYLE TYPE="text/css">
#title {position:absolute; left:15; top:0;
width:50px; height:350px; font-family:"Comic
Sans MS";
            font-size:48pt; line-height: 50%;
text-align:center;}
#text {position:absolute; left: 100; top:20;
margin-right:15%; font-size:14pt;}
</STYLE>

<BODY>

<SPAN
ID="title">M<BR>O<BR>N<BR>O<BR>D<BR>Y</SPAN>

<SPAN ID="text">
To have known him, to have loved him<BR>
After loneness long;<BR>
And then to be estranged in life,<BR>
And neither in the wrong;<BR>
And now for death to set his seal -<BR>
Ease me, a little ease, my song!<P>

By wintry hills his hermit-mound<BR>
The sheeted snow-drifts drape;<BR>
And houseless there the snow-bird flits<BR>
Beneath the fir-trees' crape:<BR>
Glzed now with ice the cloistral vine<BR>
That hid the shyest grape.
<P><SPAN STYLE="text-align:right; margin-
right:25%"><I>Herman  Melville</I></SPAN></
P></SPAN>

</BODY>
</HTML>
```

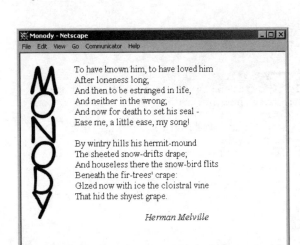

Figure 10.5: "Monody" in all its glory using Netscape Navigator 4.03

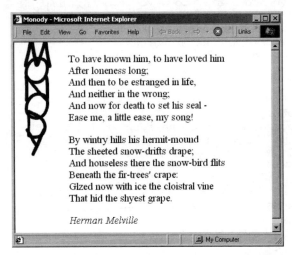

Figure 10.6: "Monody" betrayed by Internet Explorer 4.0

Given the current state of affairs, you can clearly see that it is still premature to use style sheets in a Web page.

DYNAMIC HTML

The purpose of *Dynamic HTML* is to bring HTML pages to life, allowing them to change according to the wishes of the visitor. The idea sounds great, but its implementation can be problematic because Netscape and Microsoft, as ever in competition, have chosen different approaches which are, of course, incompatible.

The Microsoft approach

This approach has the advantage of being based on W3C recommendations and does not require any new tags. It generally uses JavaScript (here renamed JScript) and has numerous specialised features. One of these, and probably the most interesting, is to make it possible to dynamically modify any property of an HTML element. Thus, `document.all.min.style.left` allows you to modify the horizontal coordinates of the object whose identifier is `min`. The coding which follows shows how, in this way, you can make two balls revolve in imitation of the needles of a grandfather clock, the outside one (`min`) advancing a fraction of a full circle for each full turn of the inside one (`sec`).

```
<HTML>
<HEAD>
<TITLE>Summary</TITLE>
<SCRIPT TYPE="text/javascript">
pi = 3.1416
degrad = pi/180
seconde = 0
minute = 0
s = -1
function pendule()
{ if (seconde == 0)
  { trotte(130, minute)
    document.all.min.style.left = x + 205
    document.all.min.style.top = y + 155
```

```
   minute += 6
    s++
  }
  trotte(90, seconde)
  document.all.sec.style.left = x + 220
  document.all.sec.style.top = y + 170
  seconde += 6
  seconde = seconde % 360

  setTimeout("pendule()", 10)
}

function trotte (r, v)
{ x = Math.floor(r * Math.cos((v-90) * degrad))
  y = Math.floor(r * Math.sin((v-90) * degrad))
}
</SCRIPT>
</HEAD>

<BODY onLoad="pendule()">
<IMG ID=sec SRC="b1.gif"
STYLE="position:absolute;  top:150;left:200">
<IMG ID=min SRC="b2.gif"
STYLE="position:absolute;  top:150;left:200">

</BODY>
</HTML>
```

Since Netscape has not implemented this type of approach involving the properties of an HTML element, the only thing that you will get if you try to load this page in Netscape Navigator is a report about the script and the display of two stationary balls side-by-side.

The Netscape approach

Netscape prefers a *layers* approach. It involves flat objects having a certain number of properties: size, colour, content, visibility. They started to appear from version 4.0 of Netscape Navigator. Three new tags were created to manage these objects. Without going any further, let's take a look at the coding below which gives the screen display shown in Figure 10.7.

```
<HTML>
<HEAD>
<TITLE>Quo non descendam</TITLE>
</HEAD>
<BODY>

<H2>Lift out of order</H2>
Once I had got to the top of the tower, I
wanted to go back down.
Alas, the lift was broken and I had use the
stairs.
<P>Ah! so many steps,
<ILAYER LEFT=20% TOP=0>steps,<BR>,
 <ILAYER LEFT=10% TOP=0>steps,<BR>,
  <ILAYER LEFT=10% TOP=0>steps,<BR>,
   <ILAYER LEFT=10% TOP=0>steps,<BR>,
    <ILAYER LEFT=10% TOP=0>steps,<BR>,
     <ILAYER LEFT=10% TOP=0>steps,<BR>,
      <ILAYER LEFT=10% TOP=0>steps,<BR>...
      </ILAYER>
     </ILAYER>
    </ILAYER>
   </ILAYER>
  </ILAYER>
 </ILAYER>
</ILAYER>

</BODY>
</HTML>
```

Figure 10.7: A long staircase to go down

Of course, in Internet Explorer, the words "steps" appear one under another and the staircase effect is lost.

Practical Advice

Here again, Dynamic HTML is shown not to be portable. If we have been brief in describing it, it is to show that this innovation has not yet come of age and the self-respecting Web author who wishes to be seen by as many visitors as possible under the best conditions should carefully avoid sprinkling it through his pages. If, however, you don't take this advice, we should point out that there is a way, using a small script, to find out whether the visitor is using Netscape Navigator or Internet Explorer. For this, you should try out the variable `navigator.appName` which gives "Netscape" for Netscape and "Microsoft Internet Explorer" for Microsoft's browser. If you want to go further, you can get the version number from the variable `navigator.appVersion` which returns, for example, "4.04[en](Win95;I)" for Netscape and "4.0(compatible; MSIE 4.01; Windows 95)" for Microsoft.

Chapter 11

Finding a host and getting yourself known

THE CONTENTS FOR THIS CHAPTER

- Finding a host
- Transferring files
- Getting yourself known

Now that you have completed your Web site, thoroughly tested it and had your friends test it locally (on your own machine and on theirs), it is time to make it known to the world at large. For this, you must first install it on a server connected permanently to the Internet. Then, you have to get yourself known. In the suburbs and in the country, when you want to hold a car-boot sale or a fête, you put up posters everywhere so that as many people as possible will be aware of the event. For a Web site, it's the same. Except that you will be putting up your "posters" across the world. It's not as difficult as you might think!

FINDING A HOST

To host your Web site, avoid using your company's server, unless you have a particularly understanding boss. Turn instead to your access provider. As we mentioned previously, most of them give you space in the order of 5 to 10 Mb on their hard disk. This is usually free, although sometimes you will be charged a small fee.

If your Web page really does attract a lot of people, the server on which it is installed may become over-loaded, or even saturated, with calls, which may lead to your 'host' taking a few measures against you such as barring access to your site or making you pay a supplement to your subscription fee.

If your access provider is not so generous or if the space offered seems insufficient, there are two solutions, depending on your budget: either find space which is being offered free or buy space on a hard disk. By going to a company which specialises in hosting Web sites, you will be able to request your own personalised domain name. The cost of domain-name registration varies according to whether you want a .com or a .co.uk domain, but companies like NetNames (**www.netnames.co.uk**) will handle the entire registration process for you at a cost of £60 to £90 for two years.

However, this is probably not the option that you will choose. If you're not fussy about the URL of your web site, you should turn to companies who provide free Web hosting to anyone who asks for it. The only catch is that most insist that you display their partner's banner advertisements on your pages. Some of these companies also offer free Web-based e-mail accounts and other services that make them worth a look.

Figure 11.1: The GeoCities home page. GeoCities offers 11Mb disk space

The best known of the "free space" providers are Tripod (**http://www.tripod.com**) and GeoCities (**http://www.geocities.com**), both in the United States. Another option is to take an account with one of the many free Internet service providers. Freeserve (**http://www.freeserve.net**) offers 15Mb web space; Virgin Net (**http://www.virgin.net**) gives you 10Mb.

TRANSFERRING FILES

Files are almost always transferred by FTP from your computer to the personal directory which has been allocated to you. Remember that a good FTP client program not only allows the transfer of files, but also the execution of certain update operations (deleting, changing names) in directories to which you have the necessary access rights.

> *Don't forget that with UNIX servers (the most widespread) the spelling of filenames must be scrupulously followed in so far as upper and lower case letters are concerned.*

The name of your home page is important. If the URL of your site is complete (for example: **http://www.myserver.co.uk/~myname/ mypage.htm**), it might not matter. But if the URL does not end with a *filename* (**http://www.myserver.co.uk/~myname/**), it must conform to the default filenames recognised by the system installed on the server, usually **index.htm**, **index.html**, **default.htm** or **default.html**. It is essential to ask your host about this or refer to its FAQ. So, to be safe, call your home page **home.htm** and put its name in your URL.

Some Web page editors (Microsoft's FrontPage or Arachnophilia – mentioned in Chapter 4 – for example) include an FTP client which automates the transfer and allows update of a site. Although not essential for sites with a simple structure, these tools allow you to save time when updating a complex site or one with many branches.

GETTING YOURSELF KNOWN

If you publish, it is with a view to being read. If you have a written publication, you also have the problem of distribution in newsagents. With the Internet, you don't have to solve this problem because distribution is automatic and free.

▬▬▬ The methods of the craftsman

As you have a limited budget, you will obviously not advertise in specialised journals but will use less costly channels.

> *A current periodical, Net@scope, offers to give you a paragraph in its next issue. For more details, direct your browser to the URL **http://www.netscope.org**.*

The paper media

If your site is a club site, you could announce your presence on the Web to your members using the written newsletter that you will almost certainly distribute to them.

Word of mouth

You could also talk about it to your friends and acquaintances. With a bit of luck you will be able to gain ground and you might interest a hundred or so people. Compared to the potential global audience on the Web, however, that is a drop in the ocean.

E-mail

If you frequently use e-mail, why not add your URL to your signature? In this way, all those with whom you correspond will know that you have a Web site. You might adopt a signature of this type:

```
George Martin
Secretary of the Society for Filling in
Blanks
          http://www.myserver.co.uk/ssfb.htm
```

This will go some way towards getting you known, especially if you subscribe to a list because, in this way, you will reach people that you don't even know who subscribe to the same list.

News

You should also give some consideration to the public poster boards of Usenet newsgroups. The same principle of advertising by using your signature may be employed. Some are even more direct in their approach, which is not always well received:

```
Come and visit my new Web site:
http://www.myserver.co.uk/ssfb.htm
```

If you take part in a newsgroup whose subject relates to your site, you might be able to attract quite a few people. In addition, there are two newsgroups reserved for announcements (although we don't get the impression that many read them):

```
uk.announce
uk.net.news.announce
```

Quid pro quo

You certainly won't be the only person interested in your subject and (especially for clubs and organisations) there will doubtless be other sites dealing with, if not the same subject, at least related subjects. Send an e-mail to their Webmaster (whose address will be somewhere on the home page of all well drafted Web pages) to ask whether you may reference his site in your appropriate section (*Other links, My preferred sites, Also look at, etc.*), on the assumption, of course, that he will do the same for you. This is a type of request that will almost always get a favourable response.

Serious methods

Generally, there are two such methods: referencing by specialised sites and referencing by an exchange in kind. We will examine a few practical ways of implementing these two methods.

Search engines

The most sure-fire way of making yourself known on a large scale is to register with search engines and directories such as Yahoo!, AltaVista, Lycos, etc. It's also worth registering with UK-only search engines such as UK Plus, UK Index and Mirago, especially if your site is particularly relevant to UK surfers.

There are many search engines and directories. How can you familiarise yourself with them? How do you choose them? How do you register with them? The answer to all these questions is simple: use a referencing service that will do the work for you.

Here again, some services are free, others must be paid for. As we are dealing with a personal home page, we will only deal with those which are free and we will only cite the best known:

- Add Me! – **http://www.addme.com.** This service will submit your site to 34 well-known (and not-so-well-known) search engines entirely free of charge.

- Submit-It! – **http://www.submit-it.com.** This service provides a free trial, submitting your site to 10 search engines. This is a taster for a commercial service covering 400 search engines.

But here again, you need to know how to present yourself and what tricks you can use to get "proper" references and have a chance of standing out among the hundreds of thousands of pages in existence.

Strategy for directories and search engines

Directories and search engines systematically send programmed automatons to find new Web sites to add to their databases. When they find something that they don't already have in their memories, they analyse it to ascertain its themes and key words. To give a weighting to these key words, they study their occurrences in the text, which can lead to some unexpected results in emphasis which the author may not have intended.

Most directories and search engines are able to exploit the presence of the <META> tag in the home page. If they find it, they then look for the attributes NAME="description" and NAME="content". By extracting the relevant information, they can supplement their databases. In the following, let's assume that you have written a Web site about beef (using, for example, the image map in Figure 8.4).

- The NAME="description" attribute should be followed by a CONTENT= attribute, after which there should be a summary of the contents of the site. In our example, this is what you might find:

```
<META NAME="description" CONTENT="Beef,
rearing, different breeds, the best cuts,
new recipes">
```

- The NAME="keywords" attribute should be followed by a CONTENT= attribute, following which will be a list of key words relating to the subject being dealt with. In our example, this is what you might find:

```
<META NAME="keywords" CONTENT="beef,
butcher's trade, rearing, bovine species,
recipes, cooking, bourguignon, miroton">
```

To increase the chances of being correctly referenced, it is good to have a clear and explicit page title (<TITLE> tag) and a first paragraph which briefly summarises the site.

If we insist on brevity in this information about your site, it is because directory databases and search engines do not provide much space for summarising the contents of a site. It is therefore better to avoid the risk of having the text suddenly cut, which might render it meaningless.

To illustrate these ideas, here is an actual example of the start of a properly constructed HTML document created by a service provider which shows that he knows his business:

```
<!-- CREATOR WEBEXPERT
     CREATION DATE: 24/03/1998
     LAST MODIFICATION: 17/05/1998
     BY: Julian Davies-->

<HTML>
<HEAD>
<TITLE>FAQ page</TITLE>
<META NAME="Author" CONTENT="Julian Davies">
<META Name="description" Content= "Bonzordis,
  Internet business !!">
<META Name="keywords" Content="Yvelines,
bonzordis, computers, Internet, Web,
hosting"></HEAD>
```

To help you to create correct META tags, you can use the HISC Taggen program. You can download a trial version from the URL **http://www.hisoftware.com**.

Two tricks to avoid

Many Web authors do not know how to write proper <META> tags and rely on indexation of the contents of their Web page by robots to get any key words. Others, wanting to be referenced from as many areas as possible, try to add key words that having nothing to do with the text but which belong to areas which are very ... attention grabbing ("X", for example). There are two ways of doing this: one is honest, the other less so:

- At the top of the home page, you can add some more or less coherent text containing a few key words that are reputedly "attractive", repeated several times (to give weighting to their occurrence), but placed in an HTML comments tag (<!-- ... -->). However, almost all robots now know how to get around this attempt to force their hand and may penalise you by simply ignoring your site.

- You can also incorporate this list of key words by writing them in a colour which is the same as the background. Figure 11.2 shows the beef home page looking quite innocent.

However, if you move the mouse cursor into the space above the title, you will see that it changes into a vertical bar indicating the presence of text. And if you select the space by holding down the mouse button and moving the cursor, the text will appear in inverse video (see Figure 11.3). The potential effect of the key words which are revealed is obvious.

This trick is also known to search engines and they generally know how to get around it.

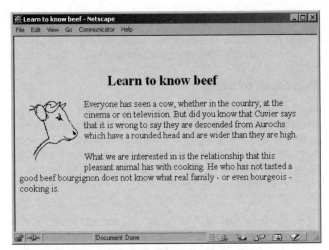

Figure 11.2: The beef page looks quite innocent

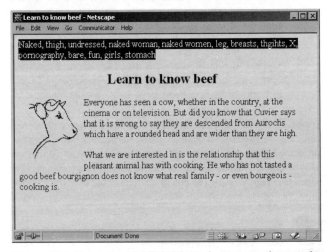

Figure 11.3: Using the highlighted words, you may hope to be indexed in areas which are more in-demand than gastronomy

Here is the text in the corresponding HTML document:

```
[...]
<BODY BGCOLOR="yellow">
<FONT COLOR="yellow">Naked, thigh,
undressed, naked woman, naked women, leg,
breasts, thighs, X, pornography, bare, fun,
girls, stomach</FONT>
<H1 ALIGN=CENTER>Learn how to know beef
</H1>
<IMG SRC="bof.gif" ALIGN=LEFT>
[...]
```

Webrings

This is a referencing system comprising a closed ring of sites with similar aims: restoring Chinese porcelain, growing wild flowers, the breeding of fish for aquaria, etc. On your home page, you place special pointers: one forwards, the other back. When a visitor clicks on one of them, he is put in touch with the central site of the Webring which chooses the 'next' site from a list of URLs depending on the direction he is moving in. If sites are added, or others disappear, update is carried out only on the central site and your page does not need to be modified. A directory lists the subject areas for which there is a ring, as well as contents for each ring. For more information, consult the Webring site at the URL **http://www.webring.com**. Figure 11.4 shows you its home page.

Figure 11.4: The home page of the Webring site

Banners

The idea of this is simple, although there are several types. A central site offers to display banner advertisements (images with a format of about 60 × 400 pixels, commercial or otherwise) on your pages. These banners contain a pointer to the Web site concerned. Each time that a visitor goes to the site thus displayed, you obtain a number of "credits". Depending on the number of credits you have obtained, your own banner will be displayed on more or fewer pages. Figure 11.5 shows you the home page of LinkExchange at the URL **http://www.linkexchange.com/**.

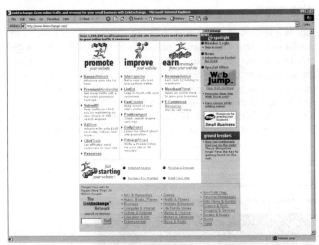

Figure 11.5: The home page for LinkExchange which specialises in banner advertisements

▬▬▬ Monitoring the success of referencing

This is where visitor counters, which we discussed in Chapter 8, come into their own. Within about two weeks, if you have taken the precaution of placing one of these counters in your page, you should notice a large increase in the number of *hits*.

Chapter 12

Useful addresses

THE CONTENTS FOR THIS CHAPTER

- Books and magazines
- Internet Resources

BOOKS AND MAGAZINES

ActiveX

- ActiveX dissected: ActiveX *From The Ground Up*, by John Mueller, Osborne, 1996.

- The active way: *Mr Bunny's Guide to ActiveX*, by Carlton Egremont III, Addison-Wesley, 1998.

General Internet

- A little about everything related to the Internet: *The UK Internet Starter Kit 2000*, by Rob Young, Prentice Hall, 1999.

- A beginner's book: *User-Friendly Using the Internet*, by Jerry Honeycutt, Que, 1998.

- A complete reference: *Special Edition Using the Internet*, by Kasser, Que, 1998.

General HTML

- HTML reference: *Instant HTML*, by Steve Wright, Wrox, 1996.

- Everything about HTML: *HTML 4 Interactive Course*, by Kent Cearley, Waite Group Press, 1998.

- The latest version: *Teach Yourself Web Publishing with HTML 4 in 14 Days*, by Laura Lemay & Denise Tyler, Sams, 1998.

- *Cascading Style Sheets: Designing for the Web*, by Håkon Wium Lie and Bert Bos, Addison-Wesley, 1999.

HTML Editors

- Microsoft's standard-setting product: *Complete Idiot's Guide to FrontPage*, by Joe Kraynak, Que, 1996.

- NetObjects' graphical editor: *Designing for the Web with NetObject Fusion*, by Stella Gassaway, Hayden Books, 1997.

Java

- Easy Java: *Teach Yourself Java in 21 Days*, by Laura Lemay & Charles L Perkins, Sams.net, 1998.

- In-depth Java: *Java 1.1 Unleashed*, by Michael Morrison *et al*, Sams.net, 1997.

- Complete Java 1.0: *Special Edition Using Java*, by Alexander Newman *et al*, Que, 1998.

- Java without programming: *Instant Java Applets*, by David/ McGinn/Bhatiani, Ziff-Davis Press, 1996.

JavaScript

- *JavaScript, The Definitive Guide*, by David Flanagan, O'Reilly, 1996.

- *Netscape JavaScript book*, by Peter Kent and John Kent, Netscape Press, 1996.

UK magazines

- Reviews about IT especially dealing with the Internet:

    > *Internet Magazine* (monthly)
    > *.net* (monthly)
    > *Practical Internet* (monthly)
    > *Web Pages made Easy* (monthly)

INTERNET RESOURCES

Most of these are Web sites, among which you will find a few FTP severs. Remember that the addresses that you find here, although they have been carefully checked, are not unchangeable. Faster than elsewhere, time brings change.

ActiveX

- **http://www.microsoft.com/france/activex/activex.htm**

CGI Scripts

- The CGI specification: **http://hoohoo.ncsa.uiuc.edu/cgi/interface.html**

- The Perl form management library: **http://www.bio.cam.ac.uk/cgi-lib/**

Visitor counters

- Available for everyone: **http://www.digits.com/**

- A site for visitor counters: **http://members.aol.com/ htmlguru/access_counts.html**
- Even more about visitor counters: **http:// www.digitmania.holowww.com/**

Copyright

- **http://www.legalis.net/legalnet**

Web Development

- The developer's station: **http://oneworld.wa.com/htmldev/ devpage/dev-page.html**
- The Web author's guide: **http://www.hwg.org/** and **http:// cbl.leeds.ac.uk/nikos/doc/repository.html**
- HTML style guide: **http://www.w3.org/hypertext/WWW/ Provider/Style/Overview.html**

Style sheets

- HTML style guide: **http://www.w3.org/hypertext/WWW/ Style/**

Drawing and Graphics Programs

- LviewPro: **http://www.lview.com**
- Paint Shop Pro: **http://www.jasc.com**
- CompuPIC: **http://www.photodex.com**
- ACDsee: **http://www.acdsystems.com**

HTML Editors and Converters

- AOLpress: **http://www.aolpress.com**
- Arachnophilia: **http://www.arachnoid.com/arachnophilia**
- Internet Assistant Microsoft: **http://www.cnet.com/ Content/Reviews/Compare/11htmleds/ss02f.html**

- SpiderPad: **http://www.sixlegs.com/spidrpad.html**

- NetObjects Fusion: **http://www.netobjects.com**

- Tools for general HTML editing: **http://www.w3.org/ hypertext/WWW/Tools/**

- Text-to-HTML converters: **http://www.yahoo.com/ Computers_and_Internet/Software/Internet/ World_Wide_Web/HTML_Converters/**

- HTML Editors: **http://www.yahoo.com/ Computers_ and_Internet/Software/Internet/World_Wide_Web/ HTML_Editors/**

Hosting Web pages

- EasySpace: **http://future.easyspace.com**

- GeoCities: **http://www.geocities.com**

- Tripod: **http://www.tripod.com**

- The Phrantic Project: **http://www.phrantic.com**

- REDCat: **http://www.redcat.org.uk**

- Netline Corporation: **http://www.netline.com**

Some Images

- Anthony's icons: **http://www.cit.gu.edu.au/~anthony/ icons/index.html**

- Barry's clip art: **http://www.barrysclipart.com**

- Clip art collection: **http://www.ist.bet/clipart/sandra.html**

- Clip art universe: **http://nzwwa.com/mirror/clipart/ index.html**

- Clip art from Yahoo!: **http://www.yahoo.com/ Computers_and_Internet/Graphics/Clip_Art/**

- GIF Wizard Home page: **http://uswest.gifwizard.com/**

- Microsoft offers: **http://www.microsoft.com/workshop/**

Image maps

- Original NCSA Documentation: **http://hoohoo.ncsa.uiuc.edu /docs/tutorials/imagemapping.html**

- MapEdit (tool for creating image maps under Windows): **http://www.boutell.com/mapedit/**

- LiveImage: **http://www.mediatec.com/**

Internet Explorer

- Microsoft's server: **http://www.microsoft.com/ie/**

Java

- One of the best-known sites about Java: **http:// www.gamelan.com/javaplatform**

- Sun Microsystems: **http://java.sun.com**

- Java as seen by Yahoo!: **http://dir.yahoo.com/ Computers_and_Internet/Programming_Languages/ Java**

- The Java Review Service: **http://www.jars.com**

- Java Developer Archive: **http://www.digitalfocus.com/faq**

- The Java Boutique: **http://javaboutique.internet.com**

- Java and Netscape: **http://developer.netscape.com/tech/ java**

JavaScript

- Netscape's server: **http://developer.netscape.com/tech/ javascript**

- An extract from UNGI by Gilles Maire: **http:// www.imaginet.fr/ime/javascri.htm**

- Planet JavaScript: **http://www.geocities.com/SiliconValley/ 7116/**

Search Engines and Directories

- AltaVista: **http://www.altavista.digital.com**
- Dogpile: **http://www.dogpile.com**
- Excite: **http://www.excite.com**
- Infoseek: **http://www2.infoseek.com**
- Hotbot: **http://www.hotbot.com**
- Lycos: **http://www.lycos.com or http://www.lycos.co.uk**
- UK Index: **http://www.ukindex.co.uk**
- UK Plus: **http://www.ukplus.co.uk**
- WebCrawler: **http://www.webcrawler.com**
- Yahoo!: **http://www.yahoo.com**
- Yahoo! UK & Ireland: **http://www.yahoo.co.uk**

Multimedia

- CoolEdit (a sound editor for Windows): **http://www.syntrillium.com**
- Indeo from Intel: **http://www.intel.com/pc-supp/multimed/indeo/ OVERVIEW.HTM**
- The MPEG FAQ: **http://www.crs4.it/~luigi/MPEG/mpegfaq.html**
- The famous QuickTime from Apple: **http://quicktime.apple.com/**
- Everything Yahoo! knows about multimedia: **http://www.yahoo.com/Computers/ Multimedia/**
- Web Review: **http://www.webreview.com**

Browsers

- Netscape's server: **http://home.netscape.com**

- General information about browsers: **http://browserwatch.iworld.com/**

Computer security

- PGP: **http://www.pgpi.com**
- Computer Security Information: **http://www.alw.nih.gov/Security/security.html**
- CompInfo: **http://www.compinfo.co.uk**

Referencing services

- Submit-It!: **http://www.submit-it.com**
- Add Me!: **http://www.addme.com**
- WebPromote: **http://www.webpromote.com**
- Web Site Promoter Resource Centre: **http://www.wprc.com**

Sources for software

- Tucows: **http://tucows.chez.delsys.fr**
- Download.com: **http://www.download.com**
- MR BIOS shareware: **http://www.mrbios.com/**
- The shareware supermarket: **http://www.shareware.com/**
- Shareware reviews: **http://www.SharewareJunkies.com**

HTML Verifiers

- Astra SiteManager: **http://www.merc-int.com/products/astrastguide.html**
- CSE HTML Validator: **http://htmlvalidator.com/**
- HTML Powertools: **http://www.tali.com/indexo.html**
- Linkbot: **http://www.tetranetsoftware.com/linkbot-info.htm**

- SiteHog: **http://www.cix.co.uk/~allied-display/redhog/**
- The W3 HTML verification service: **http://validator.w3.org/**

Web page validation tools

- Validator: **http://www.webtechs.com/html-val-svc/**
- HTMLCheck: **http://uts.cc.utexas.edu/~churchh/htmlchek.html**
- Weblint: **http://www.unipress.com/cgi-bin/WWWeblint**

HTML verification services

- Doctor HTML: **http://imagiware.com/RxHTML/**
- HTMLchek: **http://www.ijs.si/cgi-bin/htmlchek**
- KGV: **http://ugweb.cs.ualberta.ca/~gerald/validate.cgi**
- WebTechs: **http://www.webtechs.com/html-val-svc/** (United States).

Index

Creating your own Web page